PRAISE FOR
9 WAYS WE'RE SCREWING UP OUR GIRLS AND HOW WE CAN STOP

"Anea's book is really needed at this time; it not only identifies many of the root causes of the female self-esteem crisis, but provides action steps that can be taken to help empower girls. Anea is doing wonderful things for so many girls and women of all ages to help them accept who they are and be their authentic selves."
—**Stacy London, Co-Host,** *What Not to Wear*

"As women and as mothers, we need to be equipped to teach our daughters how to be confident and love themselves through all of life's ups and downs. Anea's new book teaches us how to empower our daughters to look inward for self-confidence instead of being overly influenced by today's stereotypes."
—**Fran Hauser, President of** *Time Digital*

"Anea Bogue has done the impossible: She has taken what is normally volatile and highly-charged subject matter (regarding girls, empowerment, sexuality, parental guidance, patriarchy) and speaks directly to her audience in a no-nonsense, grounded voice of female authority that calms, inspires, and guides the reader. Rather than watching our girls lose their precious confidence at the threshold of adolescence, let us join together in guiding them toward good solutions for building and keeping their self-esteem."
—**Vicki Noble, Author of** *Shakti Woman* **and** *The Double Goddess*

"Anea Bogue's new book, 9 *Ways We're Screwing Up Our Girls*, really gets to the crux of the problem as to why, even as we ride the third wave of feminism, we are still not fully addressing the needs of adolescent girls. More importantly, she gives us some practical action steps to take, so that we can finally stop talking about the problem and do something about it."

—**Kristi Meisenbach Boylan, author of *The Seven Sacred Rites of Menarche: The Spiritual Journey of the Adolescent Girl***

"Anea's book is a straight-talking, straight-shooting wake-up call for everyone who cares about women, girls, and health. It's a gem."

—**Christiane Northrup, MD, OB/GYN, and Author of the *New York Times* bestsellers, *Women's Bodies, Women's Wisdom* and *The Wisdom of Menopause***

"It is essential now that we gain a clearer, deeper, and better understanding of the roles that society and culture have played in socializing our girls, so that we can make the necessary positive shifts towards supporting their full expression and true empowerment. Their wholeness and contributions are essential to our collective future, and I commend Anea on her clear and powerful analysis. Anea's book will be helpful to everyone who reads it."

—**Jennifer Buffett, President of the NoVo Foundation and Advocate for Women and Girls**

"I highly recommend 9 *Ways We're Screwing Up Our Girls*. It is a valuable toolkit and passionate challenge for parents, aunts and uncles, grandparents and teachers—anyone who interacts with young women—to model in positive ways what it means to be a girl, and a woman, and so to positively impact our world. "

—**D'vorah Grenn, Ph.D., Director of Women's Spirituality and Author of *Lilith's Fire: Reclaiming Our Sacred Lifeforce***

"Females of all ages could benefit from Anea's expertise and how she helps empower adolescent girls and women. Girls today are easily influenced by what they see on TV and in magazines, and by what they hear on the radio, and a book like Anea's will hopefully help these young girls to be authentic and comfortable in their own skin and to not try to be something that they see in the media, which is nearly impossible to be."

—Alexandra Paul, Actress and Activist

"I founded Dailyworth.com to empower women by encouraging financial engagement and promoting the relationship between self-worth and net worth. I commend Anea on the great work that she is doing to empower women and girls. I have a daughter and am concerned about what is going on in pop culture, and about what she sees and hears. Anea's book will be a big help for many."

—Amanda Steinberg, CEO & Founder of Dailyworth.com

9 WAYS

WE'RE SCREWING UP OUR GIRLS AND HOW WE CAN STOP

9 WAYS
WE'RE SCREWING UP OUR GIRLS AND HOW WE CAN STOP

A Guide to Helping Girls Reach Their Highest Potential

Anea Bogue

Foreword by Jennifer Buffett

DUNHAM
books

DEDICATION

For my daughters, Madison Sky and Pythia.
For girls and women everywhere.
And for all those who desire a world in which men and women
are able to thrive.
We are infinitely stronger when we tap into the highest potential
of each and every person on our team.

CONTENTS

ACKNOWLEDGEMENTS

The title, *9 Ways We're Screwing Up Our Girls and How We Can Stop* actually came to me in a dream in early 2012. Almost two years later, I have completed a 43,000 word document—one that I hope will have a revolutionary impact on the way we collectively view and value girls and women. The truly extraordinary people in my life—those who cheered me on, helped me pull the pieces of the book together, and listened compassionately when the writing process had stripped me down and left me feeling broken apart—are this book's co-creators, and I will be forever grateful to them.

Thank you to my endlessly dedicated friend and business partner, Shelli Wright. Her love, commitment, faith, and investment of time and energy in me, my work, and this book, I will be "paying back" and "paying forward" for the rest of my life. Thank you to my dedicated, patient, and truly amazing assistant, Karen Fox, who researched, read and re-read drafts, until she could almost recite them. Without her to pull together the final document, when I had become too spent to do anything logistical, I might have thrown my laptop out of our third floor window. Thank you to the extraordinary Tiffany Wexler, whose belief in my work and commitment to the empowerment of girls and women inspired her to spend countless hours reading drafts and providing invaluable feedback.

Many amazing women have been a part of the personal journey that preceded this book and made it possible. Thank you to my soul sister, Kristen Olafson, who has always loved and listened to me unconditionally and with whom my vulnerability has been allowed to blossom. Thank you to Kimberly Gibbons and the women of my grad school "co-heart," who consistently created a safe space to peel back layers and gain clarity, without which I simply could not have written this book. And thank you, of course, to my extraordinary teachers Vicki Noble, D'vorah Grenn, Judy Grahn, Marguerite Rigoglioso, Dianne Jenett, and Luisa Teish. They are all pioneers who helped pave the road for my generation and have dedicated their lives to re-awakening the world to the value, equality, and full humanity of women. Their wisdom and courage inspired and guided me through what was often a painful and terrifying writing process.

It would be remiss of me to go without acknowledging, for all the same reasons, several other women who have been my teachers by virtue of their great work in the world. These include Gloria Steinem, Carol Gilligan, Deborah Tolman, Jean Kilbourne, Patricia Lynn Reilly, Betty Friedan, Eve Ensler, Lynn Andrews, Sue Monk Kidd, and Jennifer Buffett, who generously agreed to write the foreword to the book.

I must also acknowledge the truly amazing men on my team. They have worked tirelessly and usually for too little pay because they believe in this mission to create a more balanced world in which girls and women can thrive alongside their male counterparts. Thank you to my publicist, Doug Coupe, who has always gone above and beyond and definitely pulled out all the stops when it came to this book. Thank you to Steven Lewis, who played a pivotal role in the initial push to write *9 Ways* and made sacrifices along the way because of his belief in me and in my work. Thank you to Fred Palmerino and Kevin Bush, my experts for all things digital who consistently answer my "ASAP" requests and make it possible for me to connect with girls and women all over the world.

Last, but certainly not least, thank you to my family. Among the most important things my parents modeled for me were integrity, a kick-ass work ethic, and partnership between men and women. I am so thankful for these precious gifts, all three of which played a significant role in the process of writing this book and in its contents. Thank you to my brother, Todd, who I'm quite certain was my very first friend and has always been one of my biggest cheerleaders. Thank you to my smart, tenacious, and beautiful-inside-and-out daughters, Madison Sky and Pythia, whom I love so much it makes my heart hurt. So many of the lessons they have taught me inspired the words on these pages. It is my great hope that all the precious time spent researching and writing (sometimes away from them) will help to create a world in which they may thrive and one day, become change-makers in their own unique ways. Finally, thank you to my brilliant, patient, and endlessly supportive husband and partner in life, Guy Rocourt. Without him, writing this book would have been impossible—as would my ability to simultaneously be the woman, partner, and mother I strive to be.

*"What we refuse to acknowledge
we unconsciously pass on to others."*
—Bethany Webster

FOREWORD

I could say that I grew up in the 1970s and 80s as a girl in an average middle class family in the Midwest. But if I am really honest, I'd say I grew up in my late 30s and 40s after reconnecting to my authentic self, and after experiencing a larger world than the one of my youth.

My work as a global philanthropist (and feminist) has provided me a mirror that's helped me see myself, and how the world works and shapes and treats girls and women more clearly. The reality of what I have seen as common for so many girls and women around the world has shocked me to my core.

After considerable introspection and diligent inner-work, I was able to see more clearly and shift out of the diminishing and harmful socialization to which I had been exposed and succumbed to here in the United States. I claimed my voice—my *inner knowing*—a sense of deep self-respect and greater agency over my life. If only I had been supported to hold onto my self-esteem, my unique expression, and my voice from a very young age and not lost it. Yet I realize that I am one of the most privileged and fortunate women there is.

Millions of girls around the world are born with almost no chance of reaching their own unique, freely chosen potential. The world they are born into does not allow or support this. They are vulnerable to infanticide, they suffer due to lack of access to education and resources, many are forced into early marriage, and countless others are victims of sexual exploitation, violence and more. Tragically, we live in a world that preys on girls, not a world that praises them.

I felt alone growing up—just as many girls do. On top of the loneliness, I felt shame—believing that I was the only one who felt this way. I now realize that the attitudes, influences and circumstances that I faced are like a well-built, invisible computer program that runs through all of us in one way or another. This patriarchy program is in great need of a conscious and complete reboot if humanity is to set itself on a new course—one that is able to create the conditions for a more balanced, loving, co-operative and sustainable planet earth.

Our life on this planet is not sustainable if we do not begin to recognize the sacredness in life and our roles as sustainers, caregivers, co-creators and protectors—not dominators, competitors and exploiters. Society must somehow stop seeking to objectify, dominate and exploit the energies, bodies, life forces and utilities of girls and women. Every child born depends on nurturance from them, and if girls and women are not valued, safe, invested in and cherished, the implications ripple throughout humanity for generations to come.

We have become so accustomed to patriarchal thinking and behavior that we can hardly imagine what a different world would be like—one that values equally all girls and boys, and all men and women, and one that does not seek to dominate or inflict hierarchy, elitism, control, exploitation or restrictions over any other human being.

I am a living gender experiment of sort. I was born second to a twin brother in a family of two girls and two boys. My mother's typical male doctor in 1966 dismissed her "knowing" that she was pregnant with twins—to the point where the doctor acknowledged my presence only after I came into the world ten minutes after my brother. I only realized as an adult that this experience might have contributed to me feeling unseen, as though I was an "after-thought" from the very beginning. In my adult life I have worked hard to recognize this as false and to overcome it. However, I witness these feelings of invisibility playing out in many girl's and women's lives around the world today, and I see how confusing and harmful this is, and how derailing of their energy, talents, aspirations and potential.

Despite entering the world feeling somewhat "invisible," I was an outgoing and happy young girl. Girls develop somewhat faster than boys, so I learned to walk, run, blow out birthday candles, and snap my fingers, slightly before my brother did. I recall showing my brother how to do some of these things in our unselfconscious glee and excitement. Several times I recall my father or mother, intervening, holding me back in order for my brother to "go first." In these circumstances, I felt as though I had done something "wrong." From time to time, the hands would drop down and "adjust" me and put me in my proper place. There were also times when my brother and I were suddenly separated, times when he was injured, for example. I felt utterly confused, helpless, and traumatized being dismissed and separated from him without explanation—as though this didn't affect me as well. I am sure he felt the same.

At the age of four, I remember lying in bed on a hot summer night actually thinking that I could choose to be a "boy" or a "girl." My brother and I played with both girls and boys and we enjoyed playing like both girls and boys did. Anatomy didn't make any difference to us. How fun was this all! Then one hot summer night my mother stopped and reprimanded me for not having a shirt on as my brother and I played in the yard. She didn't call my brother over to put on his shirt and I was baffled. I felt ashamed and I didn't know what I had done or what was wrong with me that I needed to cover myself. I loved playing baseball with my twin and the neighborhood boys. I once pitched a "no-hitter" game to which my father reacted somewhat unimpressed. I felt a pit in my stomach at the reaction I received from him. How could it be, in this case, that I had done something "wrong?"

As I grew, I became introverted and pulled away from friends and activities. My confidence waned. I don't recall when or how it happened, but all of a sudden household responsibilities fell on me, instead of being able to spend time engaging in, or supported with my interests. My brother was not expected to share the housework. I felt insecure and unworthy in terms of needing or asking for anything from my parents, so I started to babysit and work after school at age 14. In high school after my father had teased me one too many times for expressing my opinion about something, I decided to become mute at the dinner table to "show him!" However, my plan painfully backfired. My family didn't seem to notice—or care—that I wasn't speaking. I became quieter and quieter and thinner and thinner thinking that if I disappeared, they would have to notice. But no one seemed to notice and I was further and quietly devastated.

I was always a serious student and I worked in the summers

and tried to live up to what I thought people expected of me. I felt a growing anxiety about college as I did not feel as though opportunities were for me. A growing voice inside me made sure that I knew how much I wasn't measuring up. The time to go to college came and my parents divorced. My father decided that my mother would "take the girls" and he would "take the boys." I felt like we were split up like the furniture. What did this mean? When my dad informed me he wasn't paying for my college tuition, but was sending my twin brother to college, he told me, "but you'll just get married anyway, what's the point?"

I spent an enormous amount of time on how I looked, thinking this would bring me the love and attention I craved. Yet the feelings of loneliness and despair grew in me despite efforts to appear beautiful, desirable and "okay." As hard as I tried, I could not find much honest or real affirmation of my self-worth from those around me. I strived to become some impossible image of beauty that weakened my body and spirit, and I prepared myself to be able to fit in whatever "boxes" others expected me to fit in. For many years I suffered with depression and an unclear sense of my self or my self-worth. I arranged and sacrificed myself to serve others and told myself I should be grateful in those roles. But where had I gone? Where was the authentic me? What was acceptable for me to envision or expect?

Were my parents and the people around me bad parents or bad people? No. They were fallible well-meaning people who, if they read this now, would likely not recall much of this history and would also feel deep regret. My parents, like so many parents, parented according to what society and culture expected, to what they had experienced and knew. They were not conscious of the formative negative effects they were having on me. They were guilty, but not to blame.

We are all like fish in water. And the last thing a fish sees, understands or notices is the water all around him—until he or she finds herself out of it. Patriarchy is like the water that we swim in. And although culture and society have experienced enormous changes in the past decades, the messages we give to, and that shape girls, and our ideas about girls—consciously and unconsciously—are in very real need of our attention, understanding and reform. We can no longer avoid facing or examining the deep attitudes, behaviors and influences at work that create the conditions that undermine a girl's value, voice, talent and full expression. It is time we play our critical part in creating new conditions.

This is the time to crack the thousands of years old story of an unbalanced patriarchal world. Patriarchal waters could never sustain or nourish. So it's time we get out of that water. We have an incredible opportunity before us, as so many of us become aware of the shortcomings and harm inherent in the socialization of patriarchy—to wake up like never before, heal and readjust how we think, see, and behave.

This is an internal process as much as an external one; an individual and a collective process. We know that we are inextricably linked to each other and to our environments. And here lies our greatest opportunity and responsibility—to create the conditions and environments for girls to truly thrive, so that boys and girls, and men and women may also truly thrive together. What a miraculous unfolding and transformation we will see if we rise to this occasion—and how sad our demise as a human family could be if we don't.

You have picked up an invaluable, practical book that provides real tools for understanding and meaningful change for our collective evolution—an evolution in human history inextricably linked to all girls and women being safe, seen and celebrated.

This is what we all actually need to feel. This is what we can have for ourselves and provide for future generations if we set the stage, create the conditions, and decide to do so. Then, with girls' unlocked and unleashed brilliant and dynamic potential available in the world... well, don't you want to find out?

—**Jennifer Buffett, President, NoVo Foundation, New York, 2014**

INTRODUCTION
WHAT'S GOING ON WITH OUR GIRLS?

*"Girls' self-esteem peaks when they are about
nine years old, then takes a nosedive."*
—Anita Gurian,
PhD, Child Study Center, New York University[1]

When I was nine, I felt invincible. I created an all-girl "air band" and, thanks to my very patient mother, I held rehearsals in my basement after school. Under the red lights my dad installed in front of our fireplace, the five of us belted out ABBA songs, even though we were supposed to just be pretending to sing. We even convinced the fourth-grade boys that we were touring in Hawaii on the weekends! When I wasn't rolling with "the band" I was writing, directing, and acting in plays. Once, a group of us actually performed (okay ...ad-libbed) a whole script in front of our entire student body to raise money for our school trip to Camp Arnes. I still remember getting on the loud speaker in the school office to announce that we had raised almost seventy-five dollars, thanks to the twenty-five-cent admission that everyone had paid. I had crushes on boys, but they felt recreational, not monumental. I spoke up when I had something to say. I believed in me, I believed in my potential, and I believed that I could do anything.

A year later, as I moved into adolescence, everything started to change. Every move I made, every word I spoke, and every article of clothing that I chose was second- and third-guessed. What I wanted had become secondary to molding myself to be what others wanted... especially what boys wanted. I began to make myself smaller, literally and figuratively, and I began to settle for less and less, because I didn't value myself enough to demand more. By the time I was sixteen, I was in a verbally, emotionally, and (eventually) physically abusive relationship with my first real boyfriend. I remained in that relationship for four years of my precious life. Just seven years before, I would have thought that reality impossible, as would have anyone who knew me.

Many years later, I discovered this statement in an article from the New York University Child Study Center: "Girls' self-esteem peaks when they are about nine years old, then takes a nosedive." [2] It made my heart ache. My story was not just my story. It was the story of many, and perhaps most, girls. It has been my mission since that day to understand the root causes of this devastating reality, and to create practical and effective action steps to change it.

The fact is that we have a very big problem on our hands when it comes to girls' plummeting self-esteem. From the time she is the ripe old age of ten, the average girl will begin to expend an extraordinary amount of precious life energy wondering what is wrong with her and why she can't be better, prettier, more popular, and more "perfect." When a girl walks through her daily life feeling the void created by "I'm not good enough," she will start to struggle with feelings of helplessness, anxiety, anger, and even depression. She will often attempt to fill that void and soothe those feelings with behaviors that include eating disorders, drug and alcohol abuse, risky sexual behavior, cutting, bullying, and creating unhealthy relationships.[3] These behaviors can result in deep wounds and consequences that she will carry well into her adult life.

Though the word "self-esteem" is thrown around a lot and used synonymously with the word "confidence," it is really much deeper and more complex than that. What we're really talking about is a person's sense of self-value—how valuable she feels to herself and the world. Connected to that is her awareness that she is able to act on her own thoughts, feelings and desires (personal agency), and her belief in her ability to complete tasks and reach goals (self-efficacy). Consequently, when self-esteem plummets, everything that we do can be affected and hindered in some way.

Why is it that girls' self-esteem is taking a nosedive at the age of ten? The relatively short answer is that most girls are beginning to feel the real effects of puberty right around that age. Even if she doesn't begin menstruating until she is twelve or thirteen, the hormonal changes that begin as early as age seven for girls initiate both physical and life-shaping psychological changes. Most notably, she moves into the next important phase of a process that renowned psychologist, Carl Jung, called "individuation." The process of individuation during puberty causes people to ask big questions related to self-discovery. The answers they find help to define who they are and what makes them unique and separate from their parents and others. The adolescent girl begins to ask some version of, "Who am I as a separate and unique person, and what do I need to do in order to be an acceptable, desirable, successful individual in the world?" Eager to find answers, she actively and consciously begins to search in the world around her.

In our patriarchal society, what she finds are the overt and subtle messages of female inferiority, weakness, and shame. They are part and parcel of a societal paradigm that views males as the primary authority figures and places them in roles of social, political, and moral officialdom. Many of these messages she has been receiving from the time she was little, and frankly, they are devastating to her sense of value. They often require that she abandon much of what feels good to her and what she has valued most about herself in order to fulfill society's prescription for how an acceptable, desirable, and successful female looks and behaves within the confines of the patriarchal model. Her whimsical, tenacious, unedited self must be sacrificed and replaced with someone who is thinner, quieter, and submissive in the name of accommodating the status quo. No longer does she define herself. She starts to realize that her identity, her path in life, and even her desires will be defined by someone else. She is constantly reminded that her contributions and her value in our society are less than that of males. And so begins the nosedive.

Whether you are a parent, grandparent, aunt, uncle, teacher, or coach, it is important you know that currently, the nagging "I'm not good enough" is an almost inescapable reality of being a girl today. Most importantly, it is a reality that we created and we perpetuate every day. We do so with both overt and subtle messages that tell girls that they aren't good enough. The good news is that, because we created this current version of reality, we also have the ability to create a future reality that is very different.

The bad news is that it's not going to be easy, because this problem is deeply rooted. The patriarchal norms of our culture have become solidly anchored over the course of about 3000 years. Consequently, women have been receiving the same messages and experiencing the same significant loss of self-esteem for generations.

In my one-on-one sessions with women in their twenties, thirties, forties, and fifties, from all over the country and beyond, I've found a significant shift in the way that they perceived themselves at the age of ten or shortly thereafter. One client even described "losing her voice" as she entered adolescence. One year she boldly demanded the right to audition for a solo part that had been cut from the school play…and got it. The very next year, she cried through voice lessons with her beloved vocal teacher because she suddenly stopped believing that she could sing. Most of them shared stories from right around fifth or sixth grade, when they stopped feeling good enough and started giving up pieces of themselves in an attempt to please others and feel better. The result was a loss of their sense of identity, passions, and personal desires. As they got older, more often than not, they remember settling for far less than what they once believed they would have or could have created in their lives, be it in the personal or the professional realm. For most of these women, it was their continued struggle to rediscover and reclaim the self-value that they had lost decades before that led them to seek my guidance in the first place. For many of us, once our self-esteem plummets, it rarely, if ever, returns to that earlier level without diligent work to build it back up.

Unfortunately, for generations of girls who ultimately carried their diminished sense of self-value into their adult lives, they also carried it into their role as mothers, and the cycle has continued in their daughters. More importantly, it will continue into future generations, unless we take steps to end it. I'm fiercely determined not to let this happen. I have worked hard to take back the pieces of myself that I gave up during my own adolescence, and I'm absolutely dedicated to making sure that this will not be the reality of my daughters and their future daughters.

My twenty years of experience working with girls and women in concert with my ongoing research, my role as a mother of two girls, and my own personal process of healing as a woman make up what I like to call my "reconnaissance mission." The goal of this mission has been to not only find the root cause of our self-esteem crisis, but also to identify action steps that we can take to address it. Getting to the root has required the arduous task of excavating, gathering, and interpreting information from a variety of realms: history, archaeology, religion, women's studies, sociology, psychology, neurology, gynecology, pop culture, and even the memories I carry and my daily experience as a woman. On the other hand, many of the answers, as it turns out, were hiding in plain sight and simply required that I look with a slightly different and "cleaner" lens. Even with my heightened awareness, this was necessary. Our cultural programming runs so deep that it's often difficult to see how much of our daily behavior, traditions, ways of speaking and relating to each other, religious practices, schooling, and media are all playing a role in the breakdown of girls' sense of value.

My findings have shaped the contents of this book, and I have attempted to share them in a way that is accessible, relevant, relatable, and, most importantly, action-oriented. I have endeavored to bring to light how we are (usually unknowingly) contributing to low self-esteem in girls, so we can each identify our own role in this current state of affairs. Doing so will allow us to begin to consciously create a world in which the female half of our population is consistently capable of thriving mentally, physically, emotionally, and spiritually. Why is it so important that we do so?

- Because…in the worst-case scenarios, girls are dying and, in the best-case scenarios, they are plagued with self-doubt and functioning well beneath their true potential.
- Because…for women, our deep sense of not being capable or worthy of sitting in positions of leadership keeps us from contributing to decision-making that could change the fabric of our society.
- Because…girls and women make up 51% of our population and, if we're not functioning at their highest potential, then we, as a society, are functioning at a deficit.

Fortunately, if you are a parent, extended family member, teacher, mentor, or coach of a girl, you are in a very powerful position to make a difference in her life. We can't stop the world from sending her deeply damaging messages overnight. But we can change the messages we send, we can create stronger, girl-conscious environments, and we can help her build a filter for the messages we can't control. The younger we start, the better.

And, even if she's already in the throes of adolescence, it's not too late! Honestly, I don't believe it's ever too late, or I wouldn't have worked so diligently on myself, nor would I work with so many women of all ages to heal the wounds these messages were responsible for creating in them.

How do we do this? First, we must identify the source of the problem—the messages in our society that tell our girls that they are less valuable than boys and display narrow, impossible, and demeaning standards for how a desirable woman looks and behaves. Then, we get fierce, and from a determined, loving, and protective place, we take action.

Remember that this book is dedicated to taking action. I was determined in writing this to avoid simply illustrating a dire problem and then leaving you with vague hopes for a solution. My work is always about getting to the root of the problem and then finding a set of solution-based action steps. Each of the chapters that follow this one identifies one of nine ways in which we are "screwing up our girls" and you can read them in any order that you choose. The latter portion of each chapter is dedicated to providing real-world action steps that we can take to raise girls who value themselves, who embrace the power of being female, and who are capable of filtering messages that suggest otherwise.

At the end of the day, all that most of us are missing is a clearer understanding of the problem and the tools that we need to create a solution. In the pages that follow, on behalf of girls and women everywhere, I believe I have provided exactly that.

CHAPTER 1
WAY #1: EMBODYING FEMALE INFERIORITY

"A Mother who radiates self-love and self-acceptance
actually vaccinates her daughter against low self-esteem."
—Naomi Wolf

What We're Doing

While my 17-year-old daughter seems to be working hard to *not* be like me, my 5-year-old watches and listens to me intently and subsequently imitates me in both subtle and overt ways. As she has learned to walk, talk, and just generally move about the planet, I have watched her mimic my body language, my facial expressions, the words that I say, and the way I say them (which, given my sailor mouth, can be particularly embarrassing at a dinner party). Although she is doing so less consciously now than she will when she enters puberty, from the time she started to become aware of her gender identity between the ages of two and three, she has been taking in data at home and in the world around her. It is shaping her sense of what it means to be female and how she is expected to behave in the larger world.[1]

As the most important female role model in my daughters' lives, my responsibility to them is enormous. I made a promise to each of them, upon arrival, that I would love and protect them. I also promised to do everything in my power to help them to reach their highest potential. I believe that all three of these promises are our *obligation* as parents when we choose to have children. The love and protection part comes easy for most of us. For parents of girls, however, the latter promise is much more difficult to fulfill in a world that still tells girls and women on a daily basis that they are inferior, weak, overly emotional and irrational, incapable of making responsible decisions, and lacking the capacity for leadership.

e see in the world around us shapes the ways that we see role, our value, and our potential. Therefore, it is extremely important that a girl sees examples of women who demonstrate self-value, strength, personal agency, and self-efficacy, so that she develops and maintains the same attributes within herself. She must also see societal value for women, which I will address throughout this book. *All* are essential to her ability to reach her highest potential.

This is why my number-one piece of advice to mothers who ask how they can protect their daughter's self-esteem is this: *embody the woman you want your daughter to become.* It is no different than teaching our children basic manners. If we want our children to say "please" and "thank you," be kind to others, share, and keep promises, we demonstrate these behaviors. We also diligently remind them when they fall short of these expectations. By the same token, if we want our daughters to grow into women who are self-loving, resilient, strong, independent, tenacious, confident, and courageous, we must model these qualities for them. We must show them that having such qualities is a part of being female by embodying these qualities ourselves and ensuring plenty of access to examples of other women doing the same.

I am certainly not suggesting that women are independently responsible for the problem or the solution. In the chapters that follow, I cover myriad problematic messages and what we can *all* do to create solutions. What I am saying is that we must acknowledge both the pivotal role that we are (usually unwittingly) playing in perpetuating the problem (as a result of our own programming around what it means to be female) *and* the profoundly powerful and important role that we can play, especially as mothers, in *changing* the current status quo.

Unfortunately, this is easier said than done, because, for generations, we have been programmed with absolutely absurd messages of female inferiority. Worse yet, they are so ingrained in our daily routines, traditions, religious doctrine, language, media, and more, that we often aren't even consciously aware of them – they have just become part of our cultural fabric.

In case you have any doubt that this is the case, here are just a few examples to raise your awareness:

Within Western Religion:

- God is almost exclusively spoken of as a male being, a "Father" and almighty.
- Eve, a woman, was responsible for "the fall" of "*man*kind" and, thus, for our suffering.
- As a result of this transgression, woman, it is said, is punished with the pain of childbirth (as opposed to the ability to give birth being presented as a powerful gift that makes woman a Creator and capable of sustaining the human race).
- Menstruation, a core aspect of being female, remains a taboo subject and is subtly and sometimes overtly taught to be shameful and "unclean."
- Among traditional Jewish men, it has been common practice to iterate the Talmudic "Blessed are you, Lord, our God, ruler of the universe who has not created me a woman."[2]
- The Bat Mitzvah did not exist for Jewish girls until the late nineteenth century, because women were not allowed to participate directly in religious services.[3]
- The Pope and all leaders of the Roman Catholic Church are male. In June 2010, ordination of women as Roman Catholic priests was made a "crime against the faith" by the Vatican, and churches in most Christian denominations are still led by male ministers.[4] Even Pope Francis, perhaps the most inclusive pope to date, recently reiterated that the question of women in the priesthood is "not a question open to discussion."[5]

According to the Letter of the Law:

- Until the twentieth century, a woman was considered first the property of her father and then of her husband. (The tradition of a woman taking her husband's last name upon marriage reflects this belief.)[6]
- A woman was not allowed by law to vote in the USA until 1920.[7]
- The Equal Rights Amendment (ERA), originally drafted in 1923, reads: "Equality of rights under the law shall not be denied or abridged by the United States or by any State on account of sex." The amendment died in 1982 when, once again, it failed to

achieve ratification and *has still not been ratified to date.*[8]
- Before 1976, it was legal for a husband to rape his wife.[9]
- Even as I write this, women continue to face battles to hold on to their rights to make responsible decisions regarding their own reproductive health.

In Government—In Spite of the Fact That Women Make Up 51% of the Population:
- As of today, the United States ranks 80th in the world for its percentage of women in national government, behind countries that include Cuba, Afghanistan, and Iraq. A mere 18.5% of the seats in the U.S Congress are held by women.[10]
- There has never been a female President in the Oval Office.
- Nancy Pelosi, the first-ever female Speaker of the House, did not appear once on the cover of a major magazine during her term. John Boehner, her successor, appeared on several major magazines before he had even been sworn in.[11]

In the Media:
- In a study of G-rated films from 1990-2005, only 28% of the speaking characters (both live and animated) were female. More than four out of five of the narrators were male.[12]
- On television, women make up only about 37% of prime-time characters.[13]
- The four-to-one ratio of male to female characters in movies has not changed since 1946.[14]
- J.K. Rowling, author of the *Harry Potter* series, was convinced by her publisher to go by "J.K." instead of "Joanne" because it was believed that boys wouldn't read her books if they knew that they were written by a woman.[15]

In Schools:
- The ratio of men to women presented in history textbooks is ten to one.[16]
- Of the top ten works of literature taught in high-school English classrooms today, only one, *To Kill a Mockingbird*, was written

by a woman.[17] It also happens to be the only one with a noticeably strong female main character.

- An analysis of illustrations from eighty science textbooks from both elementary and secondary schools concluded that 85% of the science professionals pictured were men. When women were pictured, they were pictured in subordinate positions to the male figures.[18]

In Our Language:

- We use the word "pussy" (slang for female genitalia and the portal through which most human beings enter the world) as a synonym for "weak."
- A coach telling his male players that they played like "a bunch of girls," for many boys, is considered the ultimate insult.

For centuries, these teachings, historic realities, and perspectives on women have sent very strong, clear messages to girls and women that their value and place in society is lesser than that of men. Although we have made some important progress in the last century, these messages are so ingrained in us and constantly reinforced through religion, various traditions, laws, politics, media, and even education that we can't seem to get out from underneath them. Passed from one generation to the next, these messages have become a natural part of our daily, collective reality. Consequently, we tend to blindly accept them as truth rather than seeing them as human interpretations and constructs that can be interpreted and constructed *differently*.

We, as women, take in these messages throughout our lives. They become a part of us and of the way that we see ourselves. Over time, we see, hear, and feel these messages so often that we begin to embody female inferiority.

So, if we don't feel valuable, confident, beautiful, and powerful, how do we embody these feelings? It's extremely challenging. And if we try to fake it (as we often do), our daughters, with their powerful intuition, see right through us. They see, just as many of us saw with our own mothers, when we self-sacrifice to the point of losing pieces of ourselves, when we tolerate being treated with disrespect, when we feel unattractive and unworthy, and when we forget the value of our own paths, contributions, and voices. As girls move closer to adulthood and they witness us accepting female inferiority, some just simply embody it themselves. Others initially feel confusion and then eventually feel anger and frustration, because they know that what we're modeling is what's in store for them.

This latter reality became clearer to me than ever when I met Sherry, a 45-year-old mother, and her 15-year-old daughter, Amy, who were experiencing a lot of tension and conflict in their relationship. In spite of the fact that Sherry bent over backwards and made obvious sacrifices to ensure that her daughter had everything she needed, drove her everywhere, and helped her with her schoolwork, Amy was often very terse with her mother. She even yelled at her on occasion, calling her "stupid." Given that Amy was a great student, mature in many ways, and presented as very thoughtful, kind and considerate, I knew there was something more going on.

I started to dig by asking Amy to list for me all the qualities that she really loved about her mother and those that she struggled with. She had no problem rattling off five or six things for the first list. When we moved on to the second list, the first thing out of her mouth was, "I hate that she is always taking care of everyone else and putting herself last." When I asked her why she would yell at her mom and call her "stupid," given that there are so many things she loves about her, this was her reply: "I just feel really angry and annoyed with her. My dad talks to her that way, too, and she just takes it. Sometimes I feel like I'm trying to get her to fight back."

A strained mother-daughter relationship was not new to me. However, it was unusual for a 15-year-old girl to be able to articulate so clearly what was really bothering her in her relationship with her mother. I strongly believe that Amy's experience is not unique, but rather, is a source of the tension and conflict that many adolescent girls feel in relation to their mothers.

The only way to end this cycle is to get to the root of our own lack of self-value and heal it. This requires that we trace to their source, those feelings of inferiority. We must identify the messages of female inferiority that we have heard throughout our lives and those that we continue to hear *and* preserve, usually unknowingly, with many of our daily behaviors. Many of us have taken some action to create greater equality in our lives and to reclaim our self-value as women. But this takes tremendous daily focus and energy when one is surrounded by messages that teach and preach the opposite. We must simultaneously work to shift something deep inside ourselves *and* transform the demeaning messages of our culture. Unless we do, our daughters and our granddaughters will continue to be subjected to them, take them, and eventually, embody female inferiority themselves.

What does it look like to embody female inferiority? Most of us are unaware of how often we actually exhibit behaviors that send a very clear message to our daughters about what it means to be a woman. Here are just a few:

- Speaking negatively about our looks, abilities, and potential
- *Not* speaking openly about or downplaying our strengths and accomplishments
- Consistently deferring to the men in our lives as "authorities" (our husbands/partners, fathers, bosses, neighbors, coworkers, etc.)
- Always aiming to please others, even at our own expense (and over time losing track of what we want because we are so focused on what others want)
- Treating our husbands' work as a priority over our own
- Expressing a lack of trust in ourselves and what we know (both intellectually and instinctively)
- Not using our voice
- Speaking negatively about *other* women
- Allowing ourselves and other women to be treated disrespectfully, especially when it comes from men
- Making time for everyone but ourselves
- Calling anything we do solely for ourselves "selfish"
- Giving up our names when we marry (While the conscious belief that woman is first the property of her father and then of her husband may not apply for many, the practice, nonetheless, implies that a woman's identity is less important than that of her male mate.)
- Giving our children their father's name and allowing our own to disappear.

The last two on this list are big triggers for many women. First and foremost, it is not my objective to shame you in any way if you made the decision to take your husband's name upon marriage. I do, however, want to encourage you to really think about the message it sends when we make it an expected norm that women surrender their name upon marriage in order to take their husband's name (which will also eventually be passed on to the children).

Both men and women are affected by our cultural programming.

It is always very telling to ask a man who is adamant about following this tradition how he would feel about giving up *his* name. I have done so and have received responses that include everything from "No way! That's my identity!" to "That's what women are supposed to do" and "I want my kids to have my name." Upon receiving these answers, the next question a woman must ask, of course, is, "What about my identity? Why is my name less important than yours?" More often than not, the answer is silence, and this speaks volumes. By the same token, many women, based on our own programming, feel that our value increases when we become "Mrs. So-and-So" or, at the very least, we want to make our men happy, so we acquiesce and the tradition continues.

Clearly, examples of the ways in which we embody female inferiority are everywhere and abundant. *This* is what our daughters see. *This* is what they see in our society. This is what *we* are modeling for them. If we don't create change *now,* the absurd notion of female inferiority *will* continue for our daughters' generation and beyond. Fortunately, there is a great deal that we can do, starting right now, to change this reality and create a much brighter future for our girls.

How We Can Stop

1. **Determine your starting place for change.** We need to determine the extent of our own programming before we can begin to reprogram ourselves and then model what it looks like to be a woman with self-authority, self-value, etc.

   - First, re-read the list that I provided of some of the devaluing teachings and messages about women in our society at the beginning of the chapter. Check in to see how many of those messages you have heard and / or can identify as having impacted your life. Think about how they have shaped the way you think and feel about being female. Writing these down may help with clarity.

• Then, complete the "Mom's Self-Assessment" that follows this chapter. It identifies ways in which we model female inferiority and will enable you to see how many of the behaviors reflect your own. Even if you're not a mom, this will be helpful to you as a woman and female role model. With both of your lists, include any additional examples that come to mind; I'd love to hear from you (info@aneabogue.com)! The more honest you can be with yourself, the better, clearer sense you will have of what you need to work on. Feeling resistance around some of them is normal. Check in and see where the resistance comes from: A sense of comfort and familiarity with the way your mother did things? Fear of conflict? Resistance to challenging or letting go of your way of making sense of the world and the unknown (religion)? Resistance to challenging or letting go of the way your family did things (traditions)? Often, when our behavior is connected to the norms of our family of origin, we will feel resistance to criticizing it, changing it, or letting it go. A good rule of thumb is to always feel like you're stretching yourself, without moving into territory that your instincts tell you you're not quite ready for. Keep journal, if you can, as you move through this process of stripping away your layers of programming. Take it one day at a time.

2. **Be confident that you are the captain of your own ship.** This is one of the most important internal shifts that you can make, because it is the one that will serve you in every aspect of this particular mission and throughout your life. In fact, I believe that it is the most important shift we can model for our daughters. We never stop being captains of our own ships. Sometimes our programming just leads us to forget that we have the ability to make wise, responsible choices from one

moment to the next. Start by pausing for just a moment and becoming conscious of choices that you make on a daily basis that shape your current life. Note the aspects of your life that you are happy with and identify the choices *you* made that created those aspects. If you are feeling frustrated or unhappy with parts of your life, identify them and become conscious of the choices you have made to create *those* realities. When you feel like you *have* to do something you really don't want to do or something that makes you feel resentful, shift your internal dialogue from "I have to..." to "I choose to..."

This may not change the initial unpleasantness of the task if you decide to do it, but it will reinforce your awareness of your active role in choosing the daily actions that create your experience and path in life. The minute this comes into focus and we own it, we hold all the power that we need to create change both internally and in the world around us.

3. **Determine what you want to create.** Once you're clear that you *can* create change, you have to become clear about *what* you want to change. Start with the most basic questions:
    - Who is the woman I want to be?
    - How do I want to feel about myself?
    - What would it look like to see myself as equal to men and to be treated as such?
    - What would true partnership with my husband boyfriend/partner look like?
    - What stands in the way of all of this?
    - What steps can I take to overcome these obstacles?

4. **Seek guidance from other wise women.** On my own journey, the biggest "aha" moments came from reading and listening to the wisdom of women whom I knew were ahead of me on this path. Their words and voices made me feel less alone and inspired me to keep pressing forward, as challenging as it often could be. For this reason, I recommend exposing yourself to the work and perspectives of other wise women. Please see the resources list below for some suggestions to get started.

5. **Commit to changing your behaviors—starting with the basics.** There are a number of behaviors on the Mom's Assessment list that we can change by simply committing to them as we would to a new morning routine with our kids. These behaviors are the ones we should enact immediately, because even small changes create important shifts and lay the foundation and momentum for more to come. For instance:

   - Commit to 60 minutes of "Me Time" every day. You can then use part of that time to read a book or watch a TEDTalk that I've listed below. ☺
   - Commit to *not* speaking negatively about yourself and about others—especially when they are not present. This is a good one for the whole family. Make it a new "house rule." This also provides a platform to speak with your daughter with regard to thinking negatively about herself and the increasingly destructive "catty" behavior she is undoubtedly witnessing and/or participating in at school.
   - Tell your friends about this commitment. It's a great way to get them involved, for themselves and for their families. It also tends to enlist their help in "catching" you when you fall back on those ingrained behaviors. Before you know it, important changes will be taking place both inside you and around you.

6. **Remember the innate power that you hold as a woman.** The good news is that we don't have to reinvent the wheel. As it turns out, the way it has been for the last 3,000 years or so is *not* the way it's always been. Women once shared leadership roles in societies. In fact, the commonly taught "reality" that a male-dominant system has always been in place is being debunked thanks, in part, to an increasing number of women becoming anthropologists and historians, and through the use of radiocarbon dating and dendrochronology. Anthropologists and historians like Marija Gimbutas, Peggy Reeves Sanday, Heidi Goettner-

Abendroth, and many others have confirmed the existence
of balanced, egalitarian, matrilineal societies that flourished
between the seventh and fifth millennia BCE, and well
before that. Why are ancient civilizations important? Because
it means that instead of forging brand new paths, we can
simply rediscover the old paths and find our way home.
It means that we don't need to invent a new version of
ourselves; we simply need *to remember who we are*. We can
tap into a time when the power, wisdom, beauty, and *value*
of women were abundantly recognized and revered, and we
can create this reality once again.

7. **Bring your men on board.** Husbands, boyfriends, brothers,
uncles *et al* all play a very important role in this mission to
heal ourselves and protect our daughters. Certainly the last
person we want to be fighting the uphill battle against is our
partner. That said, it is natural in any relationship for one
person to feel resistant and even threatened when the other
starts to make personal shifts that will affect both parties.
For this reason, communicating your intentions and sharing
your discoveries with your partner is critical. Although
husbands are primary, you can apply it to every man in your
life, by:

- Providing him with ongoing reminders of all the reasons
why you have embarked on this journey for yourself and
your daughter.

- Sharing the fact that your daughter will be inspired to
seek and create the same relationship for herself that she
sees modeled through the two of you (please see more on
this in Way #3).

- Encouraging him to read this book, if he's not doing so
already, and include him in the process. Your partner's
committed support for your efforts in private, in front of
your children, and out in public is extremely important
to your success. An invitation to be an important part of
the process, to share in the books and other resources that
you are exploring, and to co-create an environment of

equality in your home will go a long way in minimizing threatened feelings or resistance, and is likely your best shot at getting him to join the mission.

8. **Buckle up and take steps toward the bigger, deeper changes.** Each of the above steps will create great momentum for your efforts with the deeper changes. These deeper changes are the internal shifts that get to the heart of our feelings of inferiority, and it is critical that we address them if we want to create lasting change. For some women, this means working through a really dysfunctional relationship with family members, close friends, and sometimes with their partners. For many of the women with whom I've travelled on this journey, the deepest shifts come through focusing on their religious upbringing, where many of the messages of female inferiority originate. This is not to say that you must give up your religious beliefs, but acknowledging the subtle—and not so subtle—religious messages that devalue women is a big and important step in not allowing them to continue to take hold for you and your daughter. Some women will find that they cannot fully embrace both the teachings of their religion *and* their desire for self-love as a woman. Others will need to re-envision their religion (as an increasing number of women are doing) in a way that will support the notion of a Divine Feminine. Sue Monk Kidd is one such woman. She chronicles her journey and transformation in *The Dance of the Dissident Daughter* in a way that is both joyful and inspiring to read. This is a great place to start!

9. **Find or create a circle of women to be your support system.** I cannot emphasize enough the importance of surrounding yourself with women who are on a similar healing quest for themselves and their daughters. As we challenge the *status quo*, it's inevitable that we'll face some resistance in our relationships, our homes, and our places of employment. When we do, it is helpful to have a friend or two who have

been there, who know the roller coaster of emotions, and who can help to push us forward.

10. **Realize that you will need to learn, heal, and model at the same time.** We are a generation (or three) of women who are the bridge of transition to a more balanced society. Consequently, we need to simultaneously learn, heal, and model. In other words, be prepared to multitask! Don't pressure yourself with perfection. Along with being fiercely determined, allow yourself to be vulnerable. I'm a big fan of "being human" with our children (as opposed to the "I know everything and can't acknowledge my mistakes" brand). There is nothing wrong with learning as you are teaching. Indeed, there are fundamental life lessons that we offer our children when we allow them to see what it looks like to find the strength and courage to challenge the *status quo* and to create a better reality for all.

Book Resources
- *Shakti Woman: Feeling Our Fire, Healing Our World* by Vicki Noble
- *Imagine a Woman in Love with Herself: Embracing Your Wisdom and Wholeness* by Patricia Lynn Reilly
- *The Seven Sacred Rites of Menopause: The Spiritual Journey to the Wise-Woman Years* by Kristi Meisenbach Boylan (I recommend this to any woman over thirty-five)
- *Lilith's Fire: Reclaiming Our Sacred Lifeforce* by Deborah Grenn Scott
- *The Dance of the Dissident Daughter: A Woman's Journey from Christian Tradition to the Sacred Feminine* by Sue Monk Kidd
- *At the Root of this Longing: Reconciling a Spiritual Hunger and a Feminist Thirst* by Carol Lee Flinders
- *A God Who Looks Like Me: Discovering A Woman-Affirming Spirituality* by Patricia Lynn Reilly
- *The Rule of Mars: Readings on the Origins, History and Impact of Patriarchy*, edited by Dr. Christina Biaggi
- *The Feminine Mystique* by Betty Friedan

- *Women Who Run With The Wolves: Myths and Stories of the Wild Woman Archetype* by Clarissa Pinkola Estes
- *Uncursing the Dark* by Betty DeShong Meador
- *Mother-Daughter Wisdom: Understanding the Crucial Link Between Mothers, Daughters, and Healing* by Christiane Northrup, MD
- *Lean In: Women, Work and the Will to Lead* by Sheryl Sandberg

Online Resources

- Jane Fonda: "Life's Third Act" http://www.ted.com/talks lang/en/jane_fonda_life_s_third_act.html
- Sheryl Sandberg: "Why we Have Too Few Women Leaders" http://www.ted.com/talks/sheryl_sandberg_why_we_have too_few_women_leaders.html
- Shiloh McLoud's amazing art programs for women: http://www.cosmiccowgirlsuniversity.com/#

MOM'S SELF-ASSESSMENT

Am I Embodying the Myth of Female Inferiority?

Answer "true" or "false" to these questions. This is only for you. Be as honest as possible!

1. I speak negatively about my looks, abilities, and potential.
2. I don't speak openly about my strengths and accomplishments.
3. I defer to the men in my life as decision makers (my husband/boyfriend, father, boss, neighbors, coworkers, etc.).
4. I aim to please others, even at my own expense.
5. I treat my husband's work as a priority over my own.
6. I don't trust my instincts.
7. I am often afraid to use my voice.
8. I speak negatively about other women.
9. I often don't speak up when men treat me disrespectfully.
10. I make time for everyone but myself.
11. I think of anything done solely for myself as "selfish."
12. I gave up my name when I got married.
13. I gave my children their father's name.

CHAPTER 2

WAY #2: UNDERESTIMATING THE IMPACT OF DAD'S ROLE

"Don't rescue your daughter from any situation where you would not rescue your son."

—Anita Bell

What We're Doing

During a Q & A session at the end of a speaking engagement, one of the moms in the audience asked this question: "What do I do about my husband's tendency to treat our sixteen-year-old like she's still a little girl?" I was thrilled to get this question, because, typically, moms are so focused on what *they* might be doing "wrong" with their daughters, they forget about the importance of Dad's role. Better yet, I was happy for the opportunity to redefine a father's traditional role as "protector" and "provider."

My answer to her important question was this: *We need to remind any dad of three things when it comes to his daughter:*

1. He is an important role model in her life who helps to shape the way that she sees herself as a woman.
2. If he wants her to see herself as strong, independent, and capable of protecting and providing for herself, he must see her in this light and treat her as such.
3. He sets her first example for the way she should expect to be treated by someone of the opposite sex.

For most fathers, from the day that baby girl is born, the commitment to love and protect her is stronger than he ever imagined it could be, and it only grows over time. If he desires to see his daughter become a strong, confident, self-reliant woman whose sense of self-worth is not defined by her relationships with men, these three "reminders" are essential.

They will, however, require most fathers to rethink what it means to truly love, protect, and provide for their daughters.

Over the last decade, the number of stay-at-home dads has more than doubled.[1] Although moms are still the primary caregivers more than 96% of the time, there is no question that the active daily involvement of fathers is on the rise. In light of the fact that children study their familial interactions and behaviors to interpret their own place in the world, it is more important than ever for a father to have as much information as possible about his daughter's journey and the central role that he plays in her ability to reach her highest potential.[2]

Unfortunately, having seen it and learned it themselves, both in real life and in media, many dads tend to default to the "Daddy's little girl" approach to parenting their daughters—an approach that, for many reasons, achieves the *opposite* outcome.

The problem with "Daddy's little girl" behaviors and messages is that they tend to encourage the development of a damsel in distress rather than a young woman with strength, courage, and self-authority. The "damsel in distress" originated in medieval songs and tales. A knight would save the damsel as an essential part of *his* life's purpose. The damsel's weakness and helplessness enabled him to feel strong and heroic. Stories like these, reflective of patriarchal culture, have served to both define and perpetuate clear male and female roles that are "supported" by each other—the male as the hero and the female as a naïve, helpless victim in need of rescuing.

These are the qualities and behaviors of male and female characters in just about all traditional and most modern-day fairy tales, be they in book or movie form:

Males
1. Responsible for women
2. Must be rich, charming, and handsome to win the love of a princess
3. Engage in violence to solve problems
4. Must be fearless
5. Cause everything to work out

Females
1. Are passive, submissive, helpless, and naïve, waiting for the prince to appear and take control of her destiny

(It is implied that her life is not truly meaningful until she has found her prince.)
2. Focus on youthful beauty, and not intelligence, tenacity, or strength
3. Forfeit autonomy for dependence
4. Those who *are* determined, tenacious, and action-oriented are almost always portrayed as ugly, evil witches, or stepmothers trying to thwart or harm the young, beautiful damsel
5. Cannot trust other women

These stories are *everywhere,* and they are a major source of messaging that is chipping away at girls' self-value, sense of strength, courage, and personal agency. You can probably think of at least five stories off of the top of your head that still follow the "knight saves the damsel in distress and they live happily ever after" storyline—many of which you heard from the time your parents started reading you fairy tales. *Sleeping Beauty, Snow White and the Seven Dwarfs, Cinderella, The Little Mermaid*—just to name a few—*all* follow this story line and perpetuate these gender roles. We read many of the same stories to our children, which are then played out even more vividly in "family" movies, and eventually in romantic comedies and mainstream television and radio.

This programming creates narrowly defined gender roles that actually do harm to both our daughters and our sons. Our sons are basically told that they must be persistently strong, unemotional, brave, and aggressive (see the "Man Box" later in this chapter), and girls are told that being female means being the weaker sex, physically attractive, emotionally fragile, and in need of rescue by a man. "Daddy's little girl" behaviors—treating your daughter like she is a little girl well beyond her little-girl years—are often the father-daughter version of these stories and they perpetuate messages of female weakness, helplessness, dependence, and perpetual childhood.

Here are some of the most common behaviors that fall under the "Daddy's little girl" category:

- Being overprotective (If it doesn't apply to sons it shouldn't apply to daughters.)
- Treating her as fragile and helpless

- Calling her "princess" (Royalty receives deep respect and reverence. Is this what you're expressing?)
- Calling her "baby girl" (Would you use titles for your son that were associated with being helpless?)
- Dad refers to himself as "Daddy" and his daughter as "Daddy's little girl" beyond the time of her actually being a little girl (Would a fifteen-year-old son call his father "Daddy?")
- Providing everything for her, rather than helping her to develop tools to provide for herself
- Problem-solving for her, rather than helping her to develop problem-solving skills for herself (from science-fair projects to flat tires)
- Consistently making decisions for her rather than allowing her to make her own decisions
- Speaking for her, rather than providing opportunities for her to speak for herself
- Coddling her when she faces a challenge or gets "hurt" emotionally or physically, and then lashing out at the culprit on her behalf
- Not acknowledging her transition to womanhood (when she starts her period, gets her first bra, etc.)
- Continuing to speak to her and treat her like a child beyond her childhood (She enters adolescence at or around age nine.)

One of the most extreme and detrimental incarnations of the "Daddy's little girl" behavior has recently (since 1998) taken the form of "Father-Daughter Purity Balls." These formal dances, almost exclusively associated with evangelical Christian churches in the United States, are intended to promote virginity until marriage for teenage girls. Father and daughter attend together and each makes a vow. The daughter pledges to remain sexually abstinent until marriage, and Dad pledges to protect his daughter's purity of mind, body, and soul.[3] The father's role as protector and rescuer of his daughter until her wedding day is emphasized throughout the event. Not surprisingly, there is no parallel event for boys.

I've included this example mostly to make it extremely obvious that when Dad plays up the "daddy's little girl" dynamic, the message to his daughter is that she is helpless on her own and thus, both her protection and her decision making—even on a most personal level—must lie in the hands of her father and then her husband. This effectively *takes away* his daughter's ability to see herself as strong and capable of protecting herself, be it through self-defense skills or good decision-making—both of which Dad can be an integral part of helping her develop *within herself*.

To be clear, I am absolutely *not* saying that a father shouldn't shower his daughter with love and affirmation every day of her life. In fact, a father's affirmation of his daughter is directly correlated with high self-esteem.[4] I don't believe that there is a more important part of a child's healthy development and sense of value than the consistent reception of unconditional love from her or his parent.

However, truly loving our children is not about keeping them dependent on us. It is about guiding and supporting them to discover their strengths, unique gifts, and talents. *What* we affirm in them largely determines the qualities that they strive to develop. It is essential that we provide opportunities to develop tools for them to make strong choices, to ask for assistance in the right places, and to protect and provide for themselves. In short, loving our children is about enabling them to become individuals who are no longer fully dependent on us by the time they become adults. This is what it takes to raise an empowered woman—one who is complete, strong, and self-reliant because she believes in herself and her own ability to create what she wants and needs in the world.

Parents, especially fathers, tend to be diligent in doing this for their sons, so that their sons will become independent and in charge of their journey. Unfortunately, when it comes to their daughters, the opposite is more often the case, and this sends a strong message to girls, fathers *and mothers* must become aware. Not supporting our daughters in becoming loving *and* strong, vulnerable *and* courageous, partners *and* self-reliant individuals tells them that we don't believe that they are capable of being self-contained and truly empowered. Over time, a little girl starts to mirror what she learns about herself from her father's actions and words in relation to her. Being the "damsel," she starts to believe, is part of being female, and she begins to embody "damsel" behaviors. By the time she is moving through adolescence, she starts to show signs of learned helplessness. She begins seeking to become "complete" and capable of having what she wants and needs in the world, including a sense of value and identity, *through men*. [Incidentally, this feeling of being incomplete or lacking in value when one is without a boyfriend/romantic male partner is one of the most common threads among girls and women who stay in abusive relationships.[5]]

Why, then, do so many fathers default to "Daddy's little girl" behaviors?

Tony Porter, as part of his mission to end violence against women, does extremely important work with men to understand the root of many male behaviors. In what he calls the "Man Box," Porter summarizes the negative impact of our cultural programming on *men*. In it, he lists the core messages that boys and men receive about acceptable male behavior that they are expected to adhere to within the patriarchal model:

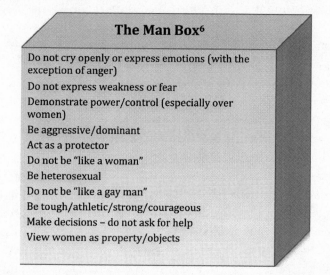

The Man Box[6]

Do not cry openly or express emotions (with the exception of anger)

Do not express weakness or fear

Demonstrate power/control (especially over women)

Be aggressive/dominant

Act as a protector

Do not be "like a woman"

Be heterosexual

Do not be "like a gay man"

Be tough/athletic/strong/courageous

Make decisions – do not ask for help

View women as property/objects

These are the values that Dad learned from our patriarchal society. From the time they were boys, most men were told and shown that following these criteria was a prerequisite for being an acceptable and successful man in our society. These patriarchal expectations shape the way that many men believe they must behave in their roles as individuals, as husbands, and as fathers. Unfortunately, in ways most of us are not fully conscious of, the "Man Box" also shapes men's perception of girls and women: as inferior, weaker, and in many ways, perpetually childlike.

Several really clear examples of this that fly beneath most people's radar (because we've totally romanticized them) are related to our marital traditions. The groom asking the *father's* permission before proposing to the bride-to-be, Dad walking his daughter down the aisle to "give her away" (Why not both parents?), the expectation that a bride will give up her identity to take her husband's name (as should their future children)—all are rooted in a perception that a woman is not an autonomous person with her own identity and personal agency. Rather, she is viewed and treated first as the property of her father and then of her husband (or, at best, as an extension of each). This is further emphasized when, in many ceremonies, the bride and groom are pronounced "man and wife"; he remains the same, unchanged, autonomous "man," while she has transitioned from being the "daughter" of one male to the "wife" of another.

The impact of these messages on girls and women cannot be underestimated. Claude Steele's work on "stereotype threat" clearly shows that, in an academic context, one's performance ability is determined not only by a person's *innate* ability, but also by the way in which one *perceives* her/his ability.[7] The latter is determined largely by the stereotypical messages one receives as defined by his/her race, sex, age, or whatever. Applied in a social context with girls, it's reasonable to conclude that for, as long as they are immersed in an environment that relays messages of their fragility, naiveté and lack of personal agency, the average girl is going to see herself in this light. She is not going to believe that she is capable of taking charge and creating her own path in the world

On this note, the way Dad interacts with his daughter *and* what she sees when he interacts with or speaks about other women—especially her mother—contributes greatly to shaping a girl's sense of herself, her role in relation to men, and her value.[8] As the "prototypical male" in her life, a girl learns quickly of her inferiority and weakness if Dad's behaviors are being informed by the programming of the "Man Box."

These behaviors may include the following:

- He speaks to or about women he works with, encounters out in the world, or sees in the media in a demeaning way. This can be as simple as making negative comments about PMS, women drivers, or using derogatory labels like "bitch" and "slut."
- He speaks about women in an objectifying way, be it through "positive" or "negative" judgments, primarily about women's appearances, that are in line with current and extreme societal norms.
- He speaks about women as inferior to men, often through reference to what roles he will support women stepping into, such as positions of leadership. (ex. a school principal, female politician, or stereotypical male profession such as a commercial pilot, chief of police, firefighter, etc.)
- He shows intolerance for assertive or aggressive behavior in women (Aggressive men are strong, while aggressive women are "bitches.").
- He expresses double standards for his son versus his daughter on matters of curfews, freedoms, responsibilities, sexual activity, and his expression of confidence in what his son is capable of doing in the world versus his daughter.
- He takes an active role in his son's activities, but not in his daughter's.
- He treats his daughter as "Daddy's little girl"—fragile and in need of being over-protected well beyond her "little girl" years.

Each of these behaviors sends strong messages about the degree to which Dad truly values and respects women as equals. And, because children naturally strive to win their parents' approval, a girl will work to define herself according to her father's expressed standards. So, for example, if Dad shows intolerance for women who are assertive or who challenge him, but responds positively to women who are accommodating or timid, his daughter is much more likely to mimic the more accepted behaviors to win her father's affection and approval. In time, if she becomes interested in boys, she will apply this learned data to winning their affection as well.

As culturally engrained as the "Daddy's little girl" behaviors may be, when a father commits to becoming aware of his own programming and consciously changing it, the floodgates of possibility crash open. As the male prototype in his daughter's life, when Dad becomes her teacher instead of her protector, by actively encouraging her to discover and exercise her own strengths and abilities, he gives her the most important gift of love and protection that he could possibly give her. Why? Because it will ensure that whether he is near or far, she will always be protected and provided for, thanks to the tools that she was given to do so for herself.

How We Can Stop (These are for you, Dad.)

1. **Work on your own programming.** For a nice, easy start, in less than twelve minutes, Tony Porter's TedTalk (listed as a resource below) will give you an entertaining and informative crash course on the reality of growing up male in a patriarchal society. It will also make clear the way that the "Man Box" is detrimental to us all. As you begin this important mission—or hone one you were already on—remember that if you don't truly make an internal shift in your perception of women (and of yourself) and embody this shift, your daughter won't buy it. The good news is that once you do, the payoff is big and will benefit you, your daughter, your son, and your wife/partner!

2. **Remember that it's never too early and never too late.** No matter what your daughter's age, there is no time like the present to make immediate changes in the way you interact with her. Become clear about the girl and, ultimately, the woman you want her to become. If you want her to have a clear sense of her female Self as strong, valuable, and capable of being self-reliant, then make a list of any of your behaviors that may be hindering this goal and, one by one, change them. The *Dad's Self-Assessment* at the end of this chapter will help you. This can be as simple, whether she's three or thirteen, as helping her become her own problem-solver rather than

"rescuing" her all the time, or making sure that, for every time you tell her that she's beautiful, you also tell her that she's strong and smart.

3. **Work in partnership as parents.** Any attempt to create change of this magnitude and importance will be much easier to commit to and accomplish if you work as a team. Once you have achieved clarity as to what your new goals are as a father, then be as clear as possible with your partner about how she can best support you. This might include establishing a signal you ask her to give you if/when you "slip," being a sounding board as you find your way through the process of deprogramming, or talking regularly about your goal with your daughter to achieve increasing clarity about your mission to raise a strong, confident girl.

4. **Learn as much as you can about girls.** Girls are wonderfully complex creatures. The more you understand what makes them "tick" (how their hormones work, how sensitive, intuitive, and passionate they can be, etc.), the better equipped you are going to be as she grows and changes over the years. I have included one of my very favorite books, *The Seven Sacred Rites of Menarche* by Kristi Meisenbach Boylan in the resource list below. It will give you a strong understanding of girls, particularly through their adolescent years.

5. **Find activities or projects that you can do together.** Help her to build a train track when she's little, or assist her with a project that she has for Girl Scouts or the science fair as she gets a little older. You can even create a project that will enable you to teach her something based on your expertise. This will enable you to accomplish three goals at one time. It will provide the opportunity for you to practice being a teacher and guide rather than her protector, she will learn a new skill, and it provides time and space for you to develop strong lines of healthy communication between you and your daughter. Always keep your goal in mind so that it guides the way you interact with her when you have opportunities like these.

6. **Teach her to be a problem-solver, rather than solving problems for her.** When she faces a problem, take the time to help her identify the problem and then find and implement solutions. When she's little, this might be as simple as *helping her* put a toy back together instead of just doing it yourself and then handing it back. As she gets older, one of the clearest examples of this is teaching her how to change a tire. If she's old enough to drive, she's old enough to learn how to change a tire. This skill will ensure that she is not left stranded on a road, forced to be "rescued" by the first strange man who drives by. *This* is what protecting your daughter looks like!

7. **Make your rules "house rules."** As you establish new rules for yourself about what you are and are not going to do with and around your daughter, making them "house rules" will bring everyone into the fold. For example, if you make the commitment to not speak negatively of or make demeaning comments about women, insist on the same commitment from the rest of your family and explain why. If you are dealing with teens, this may be met with some initial eye-rolling. But, I assure you that your daughter will be profoundly, positively affected by her awareness of your efforts and the reasons behind them. Of course, this also promises to guide your son away from any "Man Box" programming that he has been subjected to and will give him permission to be a more balanced human being who is capable of having strong, healthy relationships with women.

Book Resources
- *The Seven Sacred Rites of Menarche* by Kristi Meisenbach Boylan
- *The Paperbag Princess* by Robert Munsch (a great one to read to daughters from ages one through seven)
- *When Good Men Behave Badly: Change Your Behavior, Change Your Relationship* by David B. Wexler
- *Becoming a Dad* by Bruce Linton

Online Resources

- Tony Porter's TedTalk:http://www.ted.com/talks/ tonyporter_a_call_to_men.html
- *A Call to Men* (http://www.acalltomen.com/): Through seminars, workshops and other educational vehicles *A Call to Men* challenges men to reconsider their long-held beliefs about women, in an effort to create a more just society. We achieve this by encouraging change in the behaviors of men through a re-education and training process that promotes healthy manhood.
- *The Good Men Project*: http://goodmenproject.com

DAD'S SELF-ASSESSMENT

Part I: Am I defaulting to "Daddy's little girl" behaviors?

Answer "true" or "false" to these questions. This is only for you. Be as honest as possible!

1. I tend to be overprotective of my daughter.
2. I treat my daughter as fragile and helpless.
3. I call her "princess" and "baby girl."
4. I refer to myself as "Daddy," and to my daughter as "Daddy's little girl," even though she's no longer a little girl.
5. I tend to provide everything for her, rather than helping her to develop tools to provide for herself.
6. I frequently solve problems for her, rather than helping her to develop problem-solving skills for herself.
7. Most of the time, I make decisions for her.
8. I often speak for her, rather than allowing her to speak for herself.
9. I haven't/didn't/don't acknowledge her transition to womanhood (when she starts her period, gets her first bra, etc.).
10. I have continued to speak to her like a helpless child well after her tenth birthday (think about how you speak to your son in your desire to have him view himself as strong and resilient).

Part II: Am I showing my daughter that I believe that women are inferior?

1. I speak to or about women I work with, encounter out in the world, or see in the media in a negative way (comments about PMS, "bitchiness," or appearance).
2. I speak about women in an objectifying way (I speak and judge them mostly on their appearance).
3. I speak about men as being superior or more worthy of respect than women.
4. I make negative comments about women in positions of leadership.
5. I express dissatisfaction with women who show assertive or aggressive behavior.
6. I sometimes show double standards with my son versus my daughter on matters of curfews, freedoms, responsibilities, and sexual activity.
7. I take a more active role in my son's activities than I do in my daughter's.

CHAPTER 3
WAY #3: MODELING INEQUALITY IN OUR RELATIONSHIPS

"Equality is not a concept. It's not something we should be striving for. It's a necessity. Equality is like gravity. We need it to stand on this earth as men and women, and the misogyny that is in every culture is not a true part of the human condition. It is life out of balance, and that imbalance is sucking something out of the soul of every man and woman who's confronted with it. We need equality. Kinda now."

— Joss Whedon

"I don't want to be your other half. I believe that one and one make two."

— Alanis Morissette

What We're Doing

One of the saddest and most frustrating phenomena that I witness among teen girls is the way in which so many of them literally lose themselves in boys. I'm not talking about healthy, exciting, and invigorating young love. It's something very different from that. Every day, I work with and hear from girls who, oblivious to their own personal value, have become dependent on affirmation from their male counterparts—especially those whom they call "boyfriends."

More often than not, a girl's friendships begin to take a back seat, interest is lost in extracurricular activities that once brought her joy and a sense of accomplishment, and grades begin to suffer. Being and doing whatever is necessary to keep her boyfriend happy and close becomes paramount. Over time, she loses touch with her identity and her own personal desires, aspirations, and wellbeing. When the relationship ends, as middle and high-school relationships usually do, she feels devastated, lost, and often completely worthless.

In light of what girls see, between the archaic "damsel and knight" versions of love in fairy tales and the train-wreck relationships of "reality" television, this is not really surprising. The bar is set dangerously low for our daughters when they rarely see relationships between men and women in which both parties hold equal value and power. Worse yet, as they move through adolescence they are facing plummeting self-esteem and constant bombardment with messages that their value is defined largely by their desirability to males. All of this raises the stakes significantly for us as parents. What we model for our daughters in our own (marital) relationships goes a long way in shaping the way they see themselves and what they believe that they should expect in their relationships.

Unfortunately, most of us, thanks to our own programming, are falling short in this arena.

Over the years, it has become painfully obvious to me why adolescent girls place so much importance on their relationships with boys. From the time when they are little, girls are shown in a variety of ways that being female in our society means that your identity and value are defined by your relationship to men (father, boyfriend, husband, etc.). We do so in the most literal way when we automatically give girls their father's last name at birth (as is the case even with 92 percent of single moms, including those who *know* the father isn't going to be involved), and then again when we expect her to take on her husband's name when she gets married as an adult.[1] In my grandmother's generation, women's names disappeared altogether when they married. They became "Mrs. John Smith."

Messages of their personal value, related to this male-determined identity, come only slightly more subtly when girls see that the primary mission of most of the female characters in fairy tales and children's animated movies is to find a man, so she can *then* live happily ever after. By the time they are ten, girls are becoming privy to romantic comedies and other adult movies that take over with reinforcing these same deeply impactful messages.

All of this is very much dictated by our patriarchal paradigm, the most prevalent message of which is that power, prestige, and value are held primarily by men. Most of us were raised and socialized with traditions, belief systems, and perspectives that are rooted in and informed by this model. Consequently, our own male-female relationships almost always reflect patriarchal values. These include (but are not limited to) many marital traditions that I addressed in the previous two chapters, none of which speak to a commitment to the creation of a partnership between two whole human beings with equal value and power.

This societal programming leads us to view males as autonomous beings, so we typically teach boys to focus on their own personal achievement, establish their place in the world, *and then* find a mate. If we viewed females the same way, we would raise girls to do the same—but we don't. Instead, we tell them in a variety of ways that the only real access that they have to power in our society and the only road to happiness and fulfillment is to attach themselves to men. In doing so, we shape the way girls view relationships with men—both the importance of those relationships and the role of females within them.

Not surprisingly, being desired by and in relationship with boys becomes paramount for most heterosexual girls, especially as they enter adolescence. Meeting a standard for beauty that is often literally impossible to duplicate and highly sexualized becomes a top priority because this standard, our society tells them, is most valued and desired by men. The message that smart is not sexy, which is reiterated throughout their childhood, leads even the most academically gifted girls to start downplaying their intelligence, as early as the third grade.[2] Sports, music, and other talents that girls were once passionate about often fall by the wayside in the interest of being more attractive and more available to boys.

Sadly, many girls become victims of unhealthy relationships, because even an unhealthy relationship with a boy is better than no relationship at all, especially when you believe it defines your sense of value. These latest statistics are devastatingly telling:

- As many as one in three adolescent girls experience dating violence.[3]
- Girls and young women between the ages of sixteen and twenty-four experience the highest rate of intimate partner violence—almost triple the national average.[4]

- About 72% of eighth- and ninth-graders are "dating."[5]
- Violent relationships in adolescence can have serious ramifications by putting the victims at higher risk for substance abuse, eating disorders, risky sexual behavior, and further domestic violence.[6]
- Being physically or sexually abused makes teen girls six times more likely to become pregnant and twice as likely to contract a sexually transmitted infection.[7]
- Only 33% of teens who were in a violent relationship ever told anyone about the abuse.[8]

There is no question that the stakes are high. In light of all of the outside influences, it is essential that, as parents, we model relationships that are partnerships rather than rescue missions. We are essentially on stage 24/7, and our children are sitting in the front row. With this in mind, it is critical that we realize that, as mothers and fathers, we are modeling for our children how whole, healthy women and men act and *how they interact with each other.* What your daughter sees through your interactions as a couple, right from her early years, will shape the way she sees herself as a woman, what she expects of men, and how she sees herself in relation to them.

This is not just a wake-up call for those living the most horrendous examples of inequality in their marriage, wherein men behave as though they have permission to overtly treat their wives with disrespect verbally, physically, and emotionally. When our children are watching us intently for guidance, even the most subtle examples of male dominance and female inferiority will be seen, heard, accepted, and often imitated as normal and *expected* behaviors. Hence, even these very common examples send a strong message to our girls about the value and "place" of a woman and how she will be expected to act as a woman (Note that *both* Dad and Mom are participating in creating these messages.):

- Dad acts as the "head" of the household and has final say when household and family decisions are made, as opposed to household decisions overtly being made in partnership with Mom. This includes decisions made about finances, vacations, and children (their education, behavioral consequences, whether permission is given, etc.).

- If Dad is the primary breadwinner, Mom is given an "allowance."
- Mom frequently defers to what Dad has to say, instead of sharing her thoughts or opinions and standing by them.
- Dad is always in the driver's seat of the car when the family is out together (This may seem small, but stop and think about the literal message that it sends).
- Dad's needs are always catered to, but he rarely reciprocates for Mom when she needs the same—and she puts up with this lack of reciprocation.
- Dad makes subtle or overt expressions regarding Mom's contributions to the family as less important or less valuable than his own (whether she is a stay-at-home mom or maintains a career outside the home), and Mom doesn't object.
- Dad speaks about Mom and other women he knows, works with, or sees on television in a demeaning way and Mom does not object. This can be as simple as making negative comments about "PMS," or "bad women drivers," references to emotional expression as weak or "crazy" and, of course, references to women in an objectifying way.

It is essential that we commit to creating equality in our own relationships if we want our daughters to strive for the same in their future relationships. Many of us watched our own parents "on stage." If they demonstrated many typical, patriarchal behaviors in their relationship, without being fully conscious of it, we tend to create the same inequality in our own relationships. Patriarchy has been around for more than 3,000 years, so it's not going to go away overnight. However, many egalitarian societies existed before and, in various parts of the world, exist today. So, clearly, a different model is possible, and that model is essential if we want our girls to reach their highest potential. As with most things, this starts at home where we, as co-chairs of our household, have the greatest amount of influence and creative control.

How We Can Stop

1. **Rule as King *and* Queen of your household.** We have our
    work cut out for us when, even in a deck of cards, the king is
    often more powerful than the queen. Although you are not
    going to make changes out in the world overnight, you can take
    immediate steps in your home—the part of your daughter's
    world that matters most to her. Making the commitment to
    rule as co-heads of your household will establish a strong
    foundation for male-female equality in your home and set a
    standard that your daughter will seek to create in her future.
    Moving away from language that suggests that Dad has the
    final say on all family decisions and toward statements like
    "your dad/mom and I have decided..." will go a long way
    toward this goal. Make this commitment as a team and keep
    each other on track with a secret signal if one of you slips, so
    an immediate correction can be made (I've been known to
    squeeze my husband's leg or give him a gentle kick under the
    table and *vice versa* ☺).

2. **Make sure that your daughter sees Dad modeling respect for
    Mom and other women.** The way that your daughter hears
    her father speak about and to women, and particularly the
    way that she sees him interact with her mother, will directly
    impact your daughter's sense of herself as a woman and how
    she should expect to be treated by men. Let this be your guide
    and remember that this applies even if you and the other
    parent are no longer together. Think about the way that you
    want her to be treated as a girl (and eventually as a woman)
    out in the world, and commit to demonstrating this standard
    within your own relationship. This may require you to keep
    each other on track for a little while. I am *not* suggesting that
    Dad should be screamed at if he slips (either in reference to
    Mom or in speaking about a woman at work or on television).
    Instead, Mom should gently, but firmly, speak up on her own
    behalf (or on behalf of the woman being demeaned on some
    level), and prompt Dad to become aware of what he said. He
    can then take responsibility and adjust his statement. This

interaction will create the model of a woman speaking up for herself and a man respecting her as an equal in *hearing and responding to* what she has to say (and taking responsibility when he doesn't). If you have a son who's witnessing all the action, he's learning, too!

3. **Make sure that your daughter sees Mom modeling respect for herself and for other women.** I discussed this particular piece of the puzzle in chapter two. In the context of modeling equality in relationships, suffice it to say that a relationship between equals is rooted in the belief that women *do* hold equal value to men. If you don't believe in your equality enough to demonstrate it with your every word and action, particularly while interacting with her father, your daughter will not believe it. I have included modeling "respect" for other women here because so many of us are guilty, especially when we feel "less than," of directing our anger, frustration, and resentment at other women. Not only does this model "catty behavior," but it contributes to holding all women back when we chime in.

4. **Break gender stereotypes.** Gender stereotypes play a leading role in perpetuating inequality in our society and can limit the breadth of your daughter's dreams and development. If you want her to believe that she has value and ability equal to males and can be anything that she desires to be, she must know the power she has to make choices and have options from which to choose—from professional athlete or astronaut to stay-at-home mom or scientist. She must also be able to recognize the false limitations of socialized gender roles. Make conscious choices at home that will challenge the *status quo*. This can be as simple as Dad teaching her how to cut the grass, or seeing him contributing to housework. Mom should be just as inclined to be in the driver's seat as Dad on family outings, and her professional endeavors and contributions to the family should be overtly recognized and valued as much as Dad's.

5. **Minimize and maximize.** Take every opportunity that you get to minimize her exposure to examples of unhealthy and unequal relationships and maximize exposure to healthy relationships of equality. This includes both real-life and fictional examples that she may see through various forms of media. I will speak at greater length about the role of media in chapter six. For now, suffice it to say that teaching her to filter media messages that prescribe limiting gender roles and showcase relationships of inequality is essential to her healthy growth.

6. **Don't be afraid to acknowledge what you would have done differently.** There are many choices that we made in our early years that we look back at and today, with more wisdom and experience under our belts, wish that we would have chosen differently. My thought is that, as long as you're living, growth and change are always a possibility. I wouldn't be writing this if I didn't absolutely believe that. Your growing awareness of the patriarchal influence in our society and how it feeds inequality throughout our lives may prompt you to feel like you would have done a few things differently, both in your relationship and beyond. Nothing should stop you from changing the things that you desire to do differently. However, even *just acknowledging* with your daughter the things you would have done differently is a great way to use your experience to guide her and give her tools to make more informed choices for herself. For example, after fifteen or twenty years of marriage, it may feel like too much to consider going back to your "maiden" name or making a big leap with your husband to both hyphenate your names (for some, the ultimate demonstration of a relationship of equality). However, it takes minimal time and energy to share with your daughter that, if you could do it over, you would not have given up your name and why. This topic can easily be raised even to a really young girl by explaining why her maternal grandparents have a different last name than you and she have, or why one of her friends has a hyphenated last name.

On the other hand, if you were aware of the roots of the tradition, but you consciously chose to unite under your husband's name anyway, you can explain to her why you did so *and* let her know that she has the option to keep her name if/when she decides to get married. The key is to give her the tools to make informed choices for herself. Her capacity to do so is a fundamental part of becoming a whole human being who actively and consciously participates in creating relationships of equality now and in the future.

7. **Always keep lines of communication open.** One of my golden rules is to always do your very best to create an environment in which she feels that she can ask questions about anything and everything. Be committed to honest, well-informed answers, and value her observations about the world. A girl is not born believing that she is less valuable than a boy. This is a learned perspective that girls (and boys) eventually embody. When she sees something in the world that contradicts her instincts, she will often question it. If you support her inclination to question and to challenge the *status quo*, she will be inspired to do so throughout her life as a whole, empowered human being.

8. **Watch for signs of unhealthy relationships in your daughter's life.** From the time she is young, keep an eye out for signs that she may be involved in an unhealthy relationship. This will enable you to address the issue quickly and provide a great opportunity for your daughter to learn what red flags look like. When she's a preadolescent, most of her relationships will likely be friendships with her peers, which are often training grounds for future dating relationships. If you see signs of bullying—with her as a bully, a bystander, or a victim—ask her about it and work with other adults (parents and teachers) to support her in rectifying the problem. If she seems compelled to stay in a friendship that clearly does not make her feel good about herself or you see her molding herself to be just like her friend(s) instead of being proud of

who she is, these can be red flags that something's not right. One of the simplest tools that I use with girls is having them create a "My Relationship Criteria" list. On a beautiful piece of paper, I ask them to write down the eight to ten qualities in a relationship that are most important to them. They will typically write down things like "honesty," "kindness," "respect," and "loyalty," along with many others that may be more unique and personal to them, such as "a sense of humor." Once it's complete, I ask them to decorate it and then keep it in a special place where they can look at it often. No matter what kind of relationship they are in—friendship, familial, dating (as they get older)—this is their guideline. If a person they are in a relationship with is not meeting these criteria, they need to evaluate and make an adjustment. I encourage them to start by speaking up about their concerns and, if doing so falls on deaf ears, to distance themselves from that person to whatever extent is possible. The rule of thumb is "treat others the way you want to be treated and expect the same in return."

For girls who are a little older and have started dating, there are a whole additional set of warning signs that you should also be diligent about looking for. These include indications that the person she is in a relationship with is putting her down, acting jealous or possessive, constantly checking up on her, telling her how to dress, controlling her in various ways, or constantly expecting her to "please." Both the fact that she has chosen this relationship and the fact that she is staying in it are cause for concern. Unhealthy relationships are almost always a sign of low self-esteem. Immediately seek the help of a professional or a close family member whom you can trust if she won't speak to you about it or seems unwilling to acknowledge how unhealthy the relationship is. Do the diligent work that I suggest throughout this book to help improve her sense of self-value, so that she feels worthy of being involved in healthy relationships and expects nothing less for herself.

Book Resources

- *I Promise Myself: Making a Commitment to Yourself and Your Dreams* by Patricia Lynn Reilly
- *Rebalancing the World: Why Women Belong and Men Compete and How to Restore the Ancient Equilibrium* by Carol Lee Flinders
- *Sex at Dawn: The Prehistoric Origins of Modern Sexuality* by Christopher Ryan and Cacilda Jetha

Online Resources

- "Men, Masculinity, and Marriage" by Dr. Jaime Nisenbaum http://www.jaimenisenbaum.com/men-masculinity-and marriage/
- "Love is Respect"—a support site for dating violence, has many tools available to identify unhealthy relationships and take action to end them: www.loveisrespect.org
- National Domestic Violence hotline: 1-800-799-SAFE (7233)

CHAPTER 4
WAY #4: PERPETUATING THE MYTH OF "THE CURSE"

"How could any woman grow up in a society that hates and fears her natural, core biological function and not feel she was hiding a deep, inner flaw?"

—Vicki Noble

What We're Doing
Menstruation. Now there's a word that makes most people squirm. Our discomfort is understandable given the taboo, shame, and "ick" infused in most messages that we receive around menstruation from the time we are young.

I was reminded of just how abundant these messages are when I visited the restroom at one of my favorite restaurants the other night. Attached to the wall, right next to the toilet paper, was a dispenser for a sleek new brand of heavyweight plastic bags generously provided for women to dispose of feminine care products. They were cleverly (please be assured of my sarcasm) named "SACs," an acronym for Socially Acceptable Containment. Just as my head was about to explode, I realized that ye old "SAC" had just provided a whole new introduction to my chapter on menstruation—Exhibit A, if you will.

Let's just break this down, shall we?

"Sociall acceptable" is defined as being in line with commonly accepted standards of behavior—"people-approved," one might say. "Containment" is "the action of keeping something harmful under control or within limits."

And there you have it. This is a prime example of the profoundly negative messages that girls and women receive about menstruation throughout their lives: *A core biological function of being female, one you that will experience for approximately 3,500 days of your life, is so toxic that it must be contained, just as we must "contain" radioactive material or dirty needles.*

In fact, the very notion that menstrual blood is "gross" is possibly the greatest falsehood about menstruation. In addition to being the "lifeblood" that makes the growth of new babies possible, researchers have discovered that it has the valuable properties of stem cells. It is currently being tested for ways to cure Alzheimer's, heart disease, strokes, and other conditions. It not only helps to create life; it may save it![2]

And yet, this is just one of many examples that fly beneath our radar because we have become so accustomed to hearing them. Messages like these are among the biggest culprits in screwing up our girls and most of us are unwittingly perpetuating them. Menarche—the beginning of menstruation—is a defining experience of the transition to womanhood. Not only do our girls receive very little information about this important aspect of puberty, but the messages that they do receive about menstruation in our culture consistently portray it as dirty, shameful, and embarrassing. As a result, girls are socialized to adopt negative views about menstruation and, *therefore*, negative views about being female. Is there any wonder that the average girl lacks a sense of self-value? Or that 97% of women say that they have at least one "I hate my body" thought every day?[3]

Imagine for a moment if we taught boys, every time they turned around, that having an erection was shameful and dirty. Imagine if, in spite of the importance that erections (and sperm) hold for the continuation of our species, we socialized boys and men to hate erections so much that they actually considered taking pills that would only make erections possible just four times a year. Clearly we don't do this, nor should we. We also shouldn't do it to girls, but this is exactly what we're doing.

From a very early aged we are bombarded with messages that menstruation is to be managed, concealed, and, if possible, eliminated. We recoil for example, if our toddler finds a tampon in our purse, and we become secretive about its purpose. This sends the message that there's something shameful going on that people aren't supposed to talk about. One of my favorite admissions of this typical knee-jerk reaction came from a mom who said, "It's to stick up your nostrils when you have a bloody nose!" The mother was actually shocked by her own level of discomfort in responding to her daughter's curiosity and, fortunately, ended up telling her daughter the truth.

Earlier this year, after a presentation that I had given on keeping girls more connected to their bodies, a mom wanted to know my thoughts on her decision to put her ten-year-old daughter on a contraceptive pill. This particular pill would ensure that she only menstruated four times a year, "because no ten-year-old should have to deal with that." I asked her, with no judgment, what *she* thought she might be communicating to her daughter by telling her that having a period was something that a ten-year-old shouldn't have to deal with. She began to tear up, and I asked what her feelings had been around menstruation growing up. As her tears flowed, she said that she had always felt ashamed and embarrassed and didn't want her daughter to go through the same experience. In that moment, she realized that she was actually telling her daughter that her period was something so shameful, embarrassing, and unpleasant that she needed to take pills to make it go away. Her mission was going to achieve the exact opposite result of what she had intended.

Even in the age of the Internet, mothers are still the primary educators of girls when it comes to their bodies.[4] Unfortunately, most of us feel incredibly ill equipped because of our own girlhood experiences with menstruation. Our mothers and their mothers before them often didn't find out what was going on until the day when their first period arrived. I've heard countless stories of shock, terror, and the fear that death was upon them. Often, the extent of the explanation that they received was, "It's normal; it will happen every month until you're an old lady, and here's a box of (tampons or pads) to use."

We've inherited generations of programming that we are inadvertently passing on to our daughters. Seventy-three percent of the messages that girls receive from their mothers about menstruation are negative.[5] The good news is that girls *want* their mom to be the one they talk to about their bodies and feel disappointed when they don't.[6] This puts us in an extremely empowered position. Once we address our own programming, we can ensure that our daughters receive positive, factual, affirming information about their amazing female bodies. It's also important that Dad be well informed and involved in bringing positive energy and messaging to the subject of menstruation. Studies indicate that if Dad begins to pull away from his daughter once she hits puberty—usually because he doesn't know how to deal with it or what to say—it can have a direct impact on how she feels about herself as a woman, as well as her capacity for intimacy and healthy sexuality as she moves into adulthood.[6] In my experience, many dads *want* to be more involved but feel shut out or clueless as to how to get involved in a constructive way.

Moms *and* dads together can and must fiercely protect their daughters from negative messages about menstruation. As sensitive a subject as it may be, this includes addressing religious teachings that are harmful to her wellbeing. Most of the world's major religions have historically placed restrictions on menstruating women, and it's important to be cognizant of remnants of those teachings that have enforced taboos on menstruation. Though they are not as commonly practiced today, their very existence can significantly impact a girl when she discovers them as part of her family's religion.

For example, guided by the Book of Leviticus in the Old Testament, traditional Jewish law forbids any physical contact between males and females during the days of menstruation and for a week thereafter. Imagine how an adolescent girl might feel about her body after reading this passage:

> *When a woman has a discharge, and the discharge in her body is blood, she shall be in her menstrual impurity for seven days, and whoever touches her shall be unclean until the evening. And everything on which she lies during her menstrual impurity shall be unclean. Everything also on which she sits shall be unclean.* (Leviticus 15:19)

In Christianity, the Orthodox Catholic Church will not allow women to receive communion during their menstrual period.[8] Imagine the impact it could have for your menstruating daughter to be excluded from an important ritual because she is "unclean." Ironically, these separations from men and children and restrictions from tribal rituals were originally made by women themselves. They were menstrual-hut customs created "to protect their bodies and guarantee their *sacred* solitude" during menstruation.[9] Clearly, patriarchal religion co-opted these once sacred and self-honoring rituals and they became tools of shame and disempowerment.

In both Judaism and Christianity, the story of Eve in the garden is often associated with a menstrual "curse." I witnessed this firsthand in one of my REALgirl Empowerment Camps, after teaching a group of thirteen to fifteen-year-old girls about their menstrual "moon" cycle (in a way in which they had never heard it before). We asked if they wanted to share what they thought about menstruation before that day. Thirteen-year-old Emily said, "I always thought it was a punishment because of what Eve did and that made me really hate it. I don't feel that way after hearing what you said today, but I also don't get why someone would tell me that." It's extremely important to girls' wellbeing that we filter, reframe, or overtly reject any teaching that tells our girls that this powerful aspect of their female body—one that literally enables the continuation of our species—is a "curse."

For many of us who feel at a loss as to how to broach the subject of menstruation, we simply cross our fingers and hope that school is going to provide the information that she needs. However, only 22 of the 50 United States actually require that public schools teach sex education, and only 19 states require that *if* sexual education is provided, it actually be medically, factually, and technically accurate.[10] (Yes…you read that correctly.)

Media does their fair share of transmitting negative messages about menstruation as well. Advertisements for feminine-care products are notorious for portraying a hygiene crisis associated with periods because, after all, if they didn't convince us that there was a problem, we might not buy their product to solve it. The very word "hygiene" implies a lack of cleanliness, and commercials are often focused on concealment and secrecy. While many of these messages are so subtle that we barely realize that they're making their way into our psyches, in 2008, Midol's advertising team actually launched a marketing campaign called "Reverse the Curse!" (That was another "my head is about to explode" moment for me.)

Primetime television shows are also notorious for blatantly negative remarks about menstruation. For an example, in an episode of the police drama *Southland*, a cop says to his fellow officers over lunch,

"I don't trust anything that bleeds for seven days and doesn't die," (talking about a woman he had just started to date[11]). Keep in mind that this statement was coming from a character who was a "police officer" and, therefore, representing someone in a position of authority whom we are taught to trust. Even the most progressive television writers on some of my favorite shows seem oblivious. On *Modern Family*, Phil Dunphy refers to his wife and two daughters as "Satan's trifecta" in an episode in which all three women were in "PMS" mode at the same time. These are not the harmless jokes that we think they are, because they are seen and heard by our daughters every day and become part of the norm. This cocktail of secrecy, lack of information, and negative messages is keeping our girls under-informed and over-shamed.

They not only shape our daughter's perceptions of menstruation (and their own female bodies), but they shape *everyone's* perceptions *and* their behaviors toward women. In a 2002 study, researchers had a woman alternate dropping a hairclip and a tampon out of her bag while they recorded the reactions of the study participants around her. Both men and women rated her "less competent" and "less likeable" when she dropped the tampon than they did when she dropped the hairclip. They also tended to physically distance themselves from her if they saw her drop the tampon. The study concluded that "women's widespread concern about concealing their menstrual status is at least somewhat justified."[12] Another study showed that people who score high on the Hostile Sexism Scale also report more negative attitudes toward menstruation and menstruating women.[13]

For as long these messages are a part of our cultural fabric, girls and women will, on some level and to varying degrees, feel as though they have to apologize for being female. They will continue to expend precious energy wondering what is wrong with them instead of striving to reach their highest potential. They will struggle to love their bodies and they will struggle with eating disorders, depression, self-mutilation, and self-objectification, which often come with not loving their bodies.[14] Abundant research even draws correlations between negative attitudes about menstruation and more painful menstrual cramps, greater incidence of other "negative" premenstrual and menstrual "symptoms," and the desire to suppress menstruation altogether (in spite of the fact that the safety and long-term impact of doing so is yet unknown).[15] The negative implications of maintaining the *status quo* are far too great for us to ignore.

In 2011, I launched a brand new empowerment program for girls called REALgirl. Two of the nine modules that make up this self-esteem-focused program are dedicated exclusively to girls' knowledge of and relationship with their bodies. In 2013, I co-founded an organic tampon company called TrueMoon with my dear friend and business partner, Shelli Wright. Our mission is to provide girls and women with safer tampons *and* a more informed, positive, and healthy relationship with their menstrual cycle. I have taken on both of these massive and dedicated endeavors because, in all my years of working with girls and women, nothing has ever created a more immediate shift in the way they feel about themselves than reconnecting them with their bodies in a positive and empowered way. From nine-year-olds to fifty-nine-year-olds, and from stay-at-home-moms to female soldiers, I have seen firsthand the transformation that takes place when a girl or woman learns that her body is a powerful gift, and not a shameful burden.

Although it makes almost every parent uncomfortable initially (dads *and* moms), a really big part of building and protecting a girl's sense of self-value requires speaking about and treating menstruation as a powerful, healthy, and even magical part of being female. Unless we are actively contradicting the abundant negative messages about menstruation, our daughters will continue to be told, directly and indirectly, that menstruation, and by extension, their female bodies, are shameful—and shame makes people feel inadequate and unworthy.

And so I ask you again to consider how we socialize our boys about their bodies. The messages our boys receive about their reproductive abilities, and by extension, their "maleness," are very different than those that our girls receive. A boy quickly learns, even after a couple of embarrassing public erections, that his penis and semen are a source of virility. His "seed" is sacred, and the children his seed contributes to creating will bear his name. He learns that being male is valued, and thus, he develops a sense of pride in being a man.

What a wonderful feeling. Imagine how our girls would feel if we did the same for them.

How We Can Stop

1. **Begin with shifting your own feelings about menstruation.** We can shift the energy that we bring to the topic of menstruation by simply and logically thinking about how absurd it is to view menstruation, the cycle that literally enables the continuation of our species, as shameful. Follow this up by getting your hands on one of an increasing number of really wise books that present a very different history and perspective on menstruation. (Please see the "Resources" section for more detail.)

2. **Learn all that you can about menstruation as a powerful *cycle*.** Contrary to the common belief that menstruation is only the five to seven days of bleeding every month, it is actually a twenty-eight-ish day cycle (for some women, slightly more or less). It is a cycle during which our hormones shift slightly every day, moving us through powerful phases that we can feel mentally, emotionally, and physically. The very short version is this (Please see the "Resources" section for more detail.):

   • Our cycle begins with five to seven days of bleeding, during which time our uterus (the most powerful muscle in the female body) is shedding its lining, much like a snake sheds its skin to begin anew. Day one is the first day of our cycle.

   • At about day three, our estrogen and testosterone levels begin to rise in earnest and continue to rise throughout the first half of our cycle, as we move toward ovulation. During this time, the inclination to be out in the world, actively creating (artistically, working on projects/presentations, cooking, etc.) and interacting with others increases.

   • Once we hit our ovulation period, when an egg is released from either our left or right ovary (usually between days twelve and sixteen), we are physically charged for sexual interaction, because we are at our most fertile. This generally manifests itself as a burning desire to be out in situations that allow us to interact with those to whom we are most attracted. This is also the time when you are most likely to get pregnant if you are not taking steps to prevent it.

- After ovulation, our estrogen and testosterone levels drop, and our progesterone levels rise. As they do, our desire to move "inward" increases. We become more about ourselves and less about doing for others. When we don't honor this natural and important need to move "inward," our levels of frustration and sometimes even anger in dealing with others can heighten.

- As we near the end of our cycle, all three of our hormones bottom out and, shortly thereafter, our bleeding time begins again. This cycle happens to parallel the moon's cycle and the seasons, just to name two cycles of the universe that we, as females, "embody."

In my experience, it is impossible to know all this and still feel small, inferior, crazy, or weak. This is essential information for boys and men to understand, too. You can visit www. MyTrueMoon.com for more information and resources for yourself and your daughter.

3. **Present consistently positive messages about menstruation as early as possible.** My mother drew hearts on our kitchen calendar to mark the day when she started her period each month. For the longest time, I didn't know what the hearts meant, but I definitely viewed them as positive symbols. Consequently, when she started talking to me about menstruation, the connection between having a period and the hearts on the calendar communicated a clear, positive association. She didn't dread starting her cycle, nor did she hide it, or the hearts wouldn't have been on display in the most communal area of our home. The point is that even the smallest efforts to present menstruation in a positive light will go a long way, especially when coming from a girl's parents.

It's also important that you begin as early as possible.

I've heard moms express reservation about their daughters learning about menstruation at too young an age. They will say things like, "I just want to keep her innocent for as long as possible!" I promise you: It will not serve your daughter on any level to keep her in the dark about her body. Research shows that girls who learn about menstruation early, and in a positive way, associate it with growing up and being healthy and normal. In addition, those who are given the opportunity to communicate openly about menstruation worry less about it than girls who are not.[16]

My youngest daughter was three when she started asking questions. At five, she understands that a "blanket of blood" is created in my "belly" every month in case I want to grow a new baby. When there is no baby, the blood comes out of my "yoni" every few weeks. (The word *yoni* is a Sanskrit word for the vulva or vagina that means *"divine passage" or "sacred temple."*[17]). She has seen tampons and pads under the bathroom sink and understands that they are used to "catch" the blood. How did I know that she was "ready?" Because she asked. And had I shown signs of discomfort with her questions or maintained secrecy, she would have immediately sensed there was something "wrong." Instead, her sense is that it is all very natural—because it is. As she gets older and her capacity for understanding becomes more complex, so too will her questions and my answers.

I do want to note that it's really important to emphasize that our cycles are a source of creativity on many levels, and not just our literal ability to create babies. I believe that our capacity for creating new life is an awesome gift of being female, but every woman should feel empowered and entitled to make this very personal decision for herself rather than feeling that she is obligated to do so *because* she is a woman.

I co-wrote, with my business partner, a short book for TrueMoon called *The Essential Guide to Understanding and Loving Your Cycle.* This is a great source of information for girls and women, as well as moms and dads, and includes tips on how to talk to your children about menstruation at various ages (www.mytruemoon.com/products-tampon-kit.com).

4. **Create a Rite-of-Passage "First Moon" Ceremony.** In many ancient—and some modern—cultures, an elaborate rite-of-passage ceremony celebrates menarche, a girl's first blood. In the Navajo tradition, the *Kinaalda,* a four-day celebration of a Navajo girl upon her "First Moon," is their most important ceremony. It holds value for the whole community, because they believe that, through this rite of passage, the girl herself *becomes* Changing Woman, the great Goddess of the Navajo. With her blood, she also brings the Goddess into her family and community. For girls and women, specifically, its function in maintaining the very pulse of Changing Woman has directly impacted the reverence and status held for women in Navajo society.[18]

Modern American culture is completely devoid of a rite-of-passage ceremony that celebrates a girl's transition into womanhood upon the arrival of her period. The Bat Mitzvah is now celebrated in the Jewish faith once girls turn twelve, and the Quinceañera is an important part of Latin culture, celebrated when a girl turns fifteen. However, neither overtly acknowledges or celebrates the beginning of menstruation

Any rite-of-passage ceremony is especially powerful because it impacts all members of a community. For the adolescent, this ceremony shifts the way the "initiate" sees herself, her role, and her responsibility in her family and community, but it also signals a shift in the way in which her family and community view and treat her. Imagine how quickly we could collectively move away from the notion of menstruation as a curse if girls in our culture, upon the arrival of their first period, experienced a ceremony that honored and celebrated the power and potential that comes with their blood and with being women.

This celebration is something we can start talking about early with our daughters to create a positive anticipation of the arrival of her "First Moon." When my older daughter was nine (she's now seventeen), she was excited to make a list of guests for her impending "period party," and she associated it happily with becoming a woman. I also found it helpful to get other moms of girls on board as a way of building a collective effort and shift on the topic of menstruation so that what we were doing at home would not be immediately contradicted by the messages and energy that her friends brought to the table. I highly recommend doing so.

5. **Make sure that information and positive messages about her female body are abundant.** The most challenging part for many of us will be embracing this within ourselves. This is a wonderful opportunity to multitask. By bringing this new energy into your home for your daughter, you are also doing so for yourself. Find positive quotations about the female body and being a woman, and post them in places where she and you will see them often. Encourage her to find and post some, too. You could even research cool facts about the history of menstruation. One of my favorites is the fact that scholars believe that women were the first mathematicians because they learned to think numerically by tracking their menstrual cycles. This menstrual tracking also led women to create the first calendars![19]

6. **Introduce her to feminine-care products that are safe for her body.** Although your daughter will likely begin with pads, if she is a swimmer, dancer, or athlete of any sort, she will be asking for tampons sooner than later. When she does, it's extremely important that you introduce her to tampons that are safe. If someone offered you a plate of chlorine, pesticides, and dioxins for lunch, you'd most certainly refuse to ingest it. And yet, that is exactly what women do over 12,000 times in their lifetime by using conventional tampons in one of the most absorbent parts of the female body. A recent study concluded that: "The walls of the vagina are filled with numerous blood vessels and lymphatic vessels, which allows for direct transfer of chemicals into the circulatory system. In fact, there is considerable interest in vaginal drug delivery systems, because the vagina is such an effective site to transfer drugs directly into the blood without being metabolized first."[20]

Most women are unaware of the chemicals in conventional tampons due directly to our resistance to talk about the subject of menstruation at all. This revelation was a huge inspiration for my business partner and I to launch TrueMoon. Our mission had to involve not only providing a safer, healthier tampon but also to "Undo The Taboo," so that women will start talking about it and become more informed. There are various safe alternatives including "cup" options available in the feminine-care aisle of most health-conscious stores and on websites. Just remember that your daughter is going to be inclined to use whatever you use, so if you use tampons and haven't yet switched to organic, it's time!

Book Resources

- *Shakti Woman: Feeling Our Fire, Healing Our World* by Vicki Noble
- *Women's Bodies, Women's Wisdom* by Christiane Northrup, MD
- *Blood, Bread, and Roses: How Menstruation Created the World* by Judy Grahn
- *The Seven Sacred Rites of Menarche: The Spiritual Journey of the Adolescent Girl* by Kristi Meisenbach Boylan
- *The Seven Sacred Rites of Menopause: The Spiritual Journey to the Wise-Woman Years* by Kristi Meisenbach Boylan
- *Becoming Peers: Mentoring Girls into Womanhood* by DeAnna L'am
- *Moon Mother Moon Daughter: Myths and Rituals that Celebrate a Girl's Coming-of-Age* by Janet Lucy and Terri Allison
- *Daughters in Flower Oracle for Women and Girls* created by Itzcoatl Papalotzin, Ivonne Delgado Orea and Joanna Crowson
- *Beautiful Girl: Celebrating the Wonders of Your Body* by Christiane Northrup, MD with Kristina Tracy
- *Period. A Girl's Guide* by JoAnn Loulan and Bonnie Worthen
- *My Body, My Self For Girls* by Lynda Madaras and Area Madaras

Online Resources

- MyTrueMoon.com
- REALgirlEmpowermentPrograms.com
- Yoni.com
- "Wisdom of the Menstrual Cycle—Health Conditions and Advice:" Article by Christiane Northrup, MD: http://www.drnorthrup.com/womenshealth/healthcenter/topic_details.php?topic_id=138
- http://facts.randomhistory.com/random-facts-about-menstruation.html

CHAPTER 5
WAY #5: SHAMING HER SEXUALITY

"We teach girls shame. Close your legs, cover yourself, we make them feel as though being born female they're already guilty of something. And so, girls grow up to be women who cannot say they have desire. They grow up to be women who silence themselves. They grow up to be women who cannot say what they truly think. And they grow up—and this is the worst thing we do to girls—they grow up to be women who have turned pretense into an art form."
—Chimamanda Ngozi Adichie

What We're Doing

The most panicked calls and emails that I receive from parents are the ones that go something like this: "We just found K-Y Jelly in my daughter's room! We are furious and terrified. How soon can we see you?!"

We could replace the K-Y Jelly with any number of signs of sexual "awakening" or activity, and they would all be equally unsettling for many parents of girls. The uncomfortable and scary feelings that come up often lead us to imagine locking her in her room until she's thirty (or at least twenty-one), just so that we don't have to deal with it. Our fear leads parents to take extreme, restrictive actions that can be more damaging than they are protective because they tell her it is wrong for her to have sexual desires. We perpetuate the absurd notion that female sexuality is either nonexistent or shameful, and ultimately, we prompt her to disconnect from her body—the same one we that want her to love and protect.

Given that the healthy sexual development of our girls is an absolutely fundamental part of their healthy development overall, failing as her guides in this realm means screwing her up on multiple levels—so we need to get it together.

This is a really tough one for many of parents, because our thoughts and feelings around the subject of sex are loaded with programming. I'm going to walk us through it a little more slowly in the interest of clarity, starting with why we lose our bloody minds the minute we are faced with our daughter's budding sexuality.

In fairness, we do have a few fears on this topic that are actually natural and healthy. Looking at those first can be helpful in putting into perspective how problematic our programmed—and very unhealthy—fears are. The "natural" fears that we have regarding our daughters' sexuality are the ones rooted in facing what amounts to a huge transition into adulthood that we are not sure she and/or *we* are ready for, given the potential emotional and physical consequences that can come with being sexually active. Although it may feel like a bit of a stretch, imagine that these fears exist in the same realm as sending her off for her first day of kindergarten or to her first sleep-away camp experience.

Let's think about them in that typically more comfortable context for a moment. In either of these examples, our natural fears prompt us to wonder if she will be able to make good choices without us there to watch over her, and without us there to step in if she appeared to be in harm's way. We ask ourselves, *"Have we given her enough tools to enable her to protect herself if need be?"* What these fears don't do is prompt us to act irrationally. We wouldn't keep her home from kindergarten or never let her go to sleep-away camp, both of which are enormously valuable in her development as an individual. Instead, we would have regular, open, and comfortable conversations with her before and after the experience.

This, of course, is the most obvious way for us to accomplish three important goals of parenting, all of which are tied to each other:

- To keep the lines of communication open with our child;
- To actively guide her in the world (because no one could love her or value her safety more than we do);
- To help her develop "life tools," so that she becomes increasingly more independent of us.

Most of us have made these a regular part of our parenting, and yet we throw them out the window when it comes to communicating with our daughters about their sexual development. For a variety of reasons, we tend to default to our "programmed" fears around female sexuality. These fears are rooted primarily in what we've been taught is socially acceptable and unacceptable when it comes to female sexuality, which brings us back, once again, to "the world according to patriarchy."

First of all, our patriarchal programming leads us to view male sexual desire and behavior as legitimate and valuable, both in terms of his pleasure and "spreading his seed." Female sexual desire and behavior, on the other hand, are viewed somewhere on a scale between nonexistent and dangerous, and almost always as less valid and acceptable than that of males. These already problematic perspectives are further magnified by our tendency to view men as the subjects of sexual engagement and women as the objects. Although this is true in a variety of our societal contexts, nowhere is it as overt as in the realm of male and female sexuality. Just to be sure that we're all on the same grammatical page: The subject of any given scenario "acts," while the object "is acted upon." In the sentence "*Jane carries the book*," "Jane" is the subject doing the carrying and the book is the object, being carried. In billboards and magazine ads that show a man and a woman in a sexually charged context, the man is almost inevitably in the dominant position, actively touching, grabbing or kissing her while she stands, sits or lies there, passively receiving his action.

Accordingly, although it's not a cakewalk to deal with our sons, we tend to view and treat the advent of adolescent male sexuality as a rite of passage. Because we view a boy as the subject of his own sexuality, becoming sexually active and going after what he wants is thought to be a sign of his maturity and virility. Many parents assume that he'll just figure it out on his own, and then we cross our fingers that he won't get someone pregnant. (I recommend a much more involved approach with boys, too, by the way.) What we don't do is shroud boys' sexual activity in fear and shame.

Unfortunately, the opposite is true with girls. Remember, in the patriarchal model, men must hold absolute power. First, this means that women do not have autonomous identity or power in any context, including a sexual one. Worse yet, anyone who challenges that "absolute power" must be quickly disempowered, usually by discrediting or shaming that person. One of the most natural ways in which women threaten male "power is by inspiring male sexual desire. (For example, most high-demand celebrities will tell you that it is powerful to be desired.) One way to bring a quick end to any sense of female sexual empowerment in relation to—or, heaven forbid, over—men is by shaming girls and women with labels like "slut" or "whore" and making them *objects* of male desire to the point of dehumanizing them.

Think for a moment about how we perceive and deal with prostitution. Prostitutes are kept in business by the demand of men for sex—many of whom are married. This, the oldest profession, is also commonly thought of as the most shameful profession, and yet we say little or nothing about the men who pay for these services. She's a "whore" and he is "a man who has needs." Similarly, when twenty-year-old Miley Cyrus danced provocatively at last year's Video Music Awards show, the internet almost short-circuited with the backlash against Miley, calling her a "whore," "slut," and "tramp." Barely a word was said about Robin Thicke, her thirty-six-year-old, married-with-a child dance partner. Barely a word. We apply this same flawed programming when we deal with female sexual behavior. We disempower girls and women by making their sexuality shameful, and we have been doing so for so many generations that we don't even do so consciously anymore.

Most of us are abundantly familiar with how this taboo around women's sexual activity can play out in women's lives. We see it played out both in real life and in fictional television and movies all the time. Whether fighting for a job, in a custody battle, in a harassment suit, or even when deciding whether to use the legal system to hold accountable a rapist, women fear that their sexual past (real or fabricated by those around them) will be used to shame and discredit them. The old "What were you wearing?" question at a police precinct or in a court of law illustrates this "slut-shaming" and blaming that has been going on since the story of Adam and Eve—and it frequently leads girls and women to remain silent when they are victimized. The fact is that if girls and women were viewed and valued as autonomous individuals truly worthy of respect, they could be walking the street naked and it would not be viewed as permission to rape them. If my house is unlocked and a person opens the door to come in without my explicit invitation, he is breaking and entering. Period. If we had at least as much respect and value for women as we do for various objects of personal property, the lines of right and wrong when it comes to sexual aggression wouldn't be so conveniently "blurred."

Our programmed fears about our daughter's sexuality lie in this arena. The way in which we, as women and men, see *ourselves* as sexual beings has been determined largely by this programming, and it quickly makes its way to the surface and affects the way in which we perceive our daughters as they begin to discover and explore their sexuality. The average mom is terrified that her daughter's sexual activity will deem her a "slut," and the average dad knows that she could be objectified by boys and men, just as he was programmed to do. Both are terrified—whether they can define it or not—that this objectification of their daughter will make her a target for ridicule, abuse, rape, or worse. In some cases there is even concern about her behavior bringing shame to her family! We begin to ooze this fear from the moment we even think about our daughter's entry into this realm.

And how does all this fear impact a girl's perception of herself? There are six really big and very connected problems with all this fear swirling around a girl's budding sexuality:

1. Human beings rarely make wise choices from a place of fear. Rather, we make rash, unreasonable, extreme choices that often yield the opposite results of what we were hoping for. In this case, our fears can lead us to make poor parenting choices that fail to protect our daughters. Simply saying "no" or implementing extreme restrictions first and foremost makes her associate the feeling of shame with her sexuality. Second, it will lead her to stop asking questions and seeking accurate information about sex. This puts her at much higher risk for sexually transmitted diseases and pregnancy.[1] Third, it can prompt her to explore in more secretive, less supervised, and less *safe* settings, like the back seat of someone's car.

2. Because she will undoubtedly feel our fear, she will naturally make associations between her sexual desires and fear. Imagine if in the weeks and months leading up to her first day of kindergarten, you were exuding fear. She would naturally view going to kindergarten as something scary, and this would hinder her ability to be fully present and capable of getting the most out of the experience. In the case of her sexual development and desires, she makes the same association, and she, too, becomes more apt to make choices from a place of fear rather than ones rooted in strength and clarity. (Think: "I was afraid he wouldn't like me if I said '*no*.'")

3. With this strong message from her parents and myriad similar messages out in the world in tow, by the time she reaches middle school, she begins to face a very common dilemma. She realizes there are only two paths to choose from when it comes to her sexuality, and both are dangerous. She will be shamed for being a "prude" or a "tease" if she isn't sexually active, and she will be shamed for being a "slut" or a "whore" if she is. No matter what, she's still expected to be sexy. In either case, someone other than herself is dictating what is acceptable or unacceptable sexual behavior. This frequently leads a girl to feel a lack of power over her own sexuality, and she will begin to disconnect from her sexual desire and, inevitably, from her body. (Deborah Tolman speaks to this dilemma at length in *Dilemmas of Desire*.)

4. When a girl disconnects from her sexuality and her body, several things happen that put her in danger. She stops being the gatekeeper of her body. She stops being actively responsible for listening to what feels good and what doesn't, determining who touches her and how, and fiercely protecting herself. Instead, she explains away her sexual behavior as having "just happened" (easily explained away if she gets "drunk" first). She defers to what someone else determines feels good or doesn't, and she is much less likely to insist that protection is used if it does "just happen." [2]

5. This also sets our boys up to receive mixed messages they are underprepared to interpret. When a girl doesn't feel like she can own her sexuality and be in charge of her sexual desires *without shame*, she will expect the boy to take the lead. This can prompt a boy to think that he has permission to go way further than he actually does. Couple that with the societal ("Man Box") message that he is supposed to be dominant and that he's a "faggot" if he's not, and you've got a recipe for sexual aggression. Current studies show that as many as one in three high school girls has been sexually assaulted by a dating partner.[3] None of us wants this for our daughters, nor do we want our sons to learn about this sexual dilemma through a rape charge.

6. Lastly, all this fear, feeding on itself and growing, leads us to over-manage and under-value female sexuality. We perpetuate the shaming and subject our girls *and our boys* to the same programming that has been passed from generation to generation—and once again, the cycle continues.

The impact that these fears have on a girl's development—sexual, psychological, physical, and emotional—is extremely detrimental and there is a strong likelihood that she will carry this disconnection from a core part of her being well into adulthood. We simply cannot underestimate how important it is that we ensure that she has every opportunity to become a well-informed, shame-free, sexual being. According to the classic *Handbook of Adolescent Development*, one must become a "self-motivated sexual actor" as part of her/his overall development.[4]

In 2001, U.S. Surgeon General David Satcher suggested that "it is necessary to appreciate what sexual health is, that it is connected with both physical and mental health, and that it is important throughout the entire lifespan, not just in the reproductive years."[5] Exploration in the sexual arena is clearly as important as any other for the development of her sense of personal agency, value *and* healthy, vivacious sexuality. The cultural messages that she receives about female sexuality will substantially influence that journey and its outcome. Back in 1948, anthropologist Margaret Mead did an extensive study of seven ethnic groups in the Pacific islands. She determined that a woman's sexual fulfillment and the positive meaning of her sexuality in her own mind depend on whether her culture recognizes female desire as valuable and whether her culture allows her to understand her sexual anatomy.[6]

It is essential for our daughters' healthy development that we shift out of the programming that perpetuates shaming, and begin guiding our girls to discover, embrace, and remain in charge of their own sexuality. This is absolutely critical if we hope to raise girls who are valued and value themselves. Simply put, every girl must be encouraged and allowed to be *the subject of her own desire* rather than the object of someone else's. I believe that this is what we all want as parents of girls. And I believe that if more parents realized that our fear-based attempts to "protect" them actually yield the opposite results, we would very quickly and collectively change our approach.

How We Can Stop

1. **Remember that we are all responsible for creating change.** The patriarchal model is a human construct. We created it; we can change it. This is a fundamental shift in our thinking that should prompt us to question how our current cultural model affects our daughters' (and our sons) healthy sexual development and how we can get busy changing it. Turn on this switch of awareness within yourself and get busy!

2. **Move beyond your own programming.** Remember that it is critical for us to embody what we want our daughters to become. Your own issues with shame and sexuality will inevitably show in the way in which you speak about sex. If you don't believe what you're saying, your daughter definitely won't. I list several great books on this subject at the end of this chapter. There are also a burgeoning number of therapists who specialize in human sexuality and can assist with pulling back layers of programming to get to a healthier, more connected sexual state. This applies to Mom *and* Dad and will certainly pay off for you and your kids!

3. **Keep in mind your three fundamental parenting goals, and prepare for slight variations.** Your goals and basic steps to achieving those goals as parents should remain the same, even when it comes to guiding and supporting your daughter through her development as a sexual being. It is essential that you keep the lines of communication open, continue to actively guide her in the world, and help her develop tools for strong, self-honoring decision-making in all aspects of her life. This is how any human being learns that s/he has the right and ability to act in the world on their own behalf. Remember that the goal is to help her become increasingly *more independent of you.*

   If your daughter is already well into adolescence (thirteen or older), it will be more challenging to suddenly open the lines of communication in the realm of sexuality. But it's not impossible. Be persistent and enlist the help of another trusted adult with a healthy perspective on sexuality. This can be an aunt or adult friend whom your daughter trusts, respects, and has a rapport with. A counselor, therapist, or life coach who specializes in teen girls is another excellent option. Just be sure to pre-screen this person to ensure that it isn't someone still totally entrenched in patriarchal programming.

4. **Begin her sexual education as early as her questions demand.** I firmly believe that if we listen closely, our children will tell us when they are ready to know about something new that they have discovered. Granted, in our age of "everywhere media," her questions will likely come up much earlier than you had imagined. This just means that you need to be ready; otherwise, her guidance will come solely from "out there." The best answer is always one that is honest, age-appropriate, and fearless. Start by avoiding silly pseudonyms for genitalia. We don't call an arm by another name because there's nothing shameful or secretive about an arm. There also shouldn't be anything shameful about her genitalia and researchers have found an increase in self-esteem and comfort when girls were provided with actual names for their female body parts.[7]

Words like "vagina," "vulva" or "yoni" are all great options and should be used from the very beginning. If you notice her exploring her body (as *all kids do*), *don't* shame her. It is totally natural, normal, and healthy for kids, even from the time when they are babies, to touch their genitals. When they discover that it feels good, they want to do it more. Just encourage her to have her special private time with her body when she's alone in her room. Remember, we want her to know her body very well. This will help her stay in charge of it when she gets to an age when she chooses to share it with someone else.

When she does begin asking questions, it's okay if you have to buy yourself some time to clear your head. Just say: "That's a really good question! I'd really like to think about how best to answer that. Can we talk about it before bed tonight?" This approach is infinitely better than shutting her down because *you* are uncomfortable with the question. I assure you that, if she doesn't get an answer from you, she'll go looking for it elsewhere, and, more often than not, it won't be the informed, responsible answer that you can commit to providing. I've provided some resources below to guide you.

5. **Banish the word "slut" from your household.** Every time I hear someone use this word, I ask what they think that person has done to deem her a "slut." Most of the time, the word is being used to shame, belittle, and disempower a girl or woman who has either dared to explore or express her sexuality and/or is desired by—i.e., popular with—the opposite sex. It has become the quintessential word for shaming female sexuality and is used excessively and brutally to disempower girls and women. We directly contribute to this programming and cycle for as long as we continue to use it. Explaining to your kids why it is off-limits makes a strong statement. It is also a great teaching tool that may even save lives. Multiple girls have committed suicide after being relentlessly "slut-shamed" by their peers, both in person and via social media. Girls like Phoebe Prince, Ashlynn Connor,

Amanda Todd, and Felicia Garcia, to name a few, took their own lives because of relentless torment and slut-shaming by their classmates. Some were as young as ten years old.[8]

6. **Bring your "boys" into the conversation.** It is essential that a girl's father (or father figure) be part of this effort, if at all possible. Dad's behavior and his expressed opinions on female sexuality will set a standard for what his daughter should expect and tolerate from the opposite sex. This is also true of brothers, especially older ones. The double standard that men carry for women in their lives—one for their mothers/sisters/wives/daughters and then another for the rest of womankind—has to stop for our sake and for theirs. Addressing the objectification and sexual shaming of girls by putting your daughter's face on the issue will bring it into sharp focus for them. Look what it did for rapper Jay-Z, who announced that he would no longer use the word "bitches" to refer to women in his lyrics *just days* after his baby girl was born.

   It's also important that we all work together to dispel the myth of male weakness. This is the idea that men are too weak to control themselves sexually when they are around women. This places all responsibility on girls and women to ward off male sexual advances, instead of holding men accountable for their own behavior. This is more than any girl or woman should have to carry, and it's insulting to men.

7. **Avoid double standards with your daughters and sons.** It sends a very clear message about female sexuality being shameful and dangerous and male sexuality being safe, normal, and healthy when we have different standards, curfews, conversations, and degrees of "protective" measures for our daughters and our sons. When your son is being patted on the back for being a "lady's man," but you are intolerant of your daughter having multiple boyfriends throughout high school, the programming is being perpetuated and damage is being done. Catch yourself (and others) when you become aware, and correct it quickly and openly with your kids.

8. **Remember the role of self-esteem.** Study after study tells us that girls with low self-esteem tend to have sex earlier and without protection.[9] They do so because they are feeling desperate for validation, primarily through male attention, to make them feel more valued. In other words, they are making the choice to have sex from a place of weakness rather than from a place of strength. In my REALgirl Empowerment workshops and camps, we teach every girl that her body is *her* temple and that *she* is the gatekeeper. This applies to eating healthy food, exercising, and not allowing people who make her feel bad about herself to be near or "enter" the temple. It also means that *she* determines who touches her, as well as when, where, how, and to what extent. This is a core lesson in self-value and one that is important to instill in your daughter as early as possible. It *does not* mean telling her that her body is sacred and must be saved for her husband, as this again reinforces the notion that her body belongs to someone else and its value is measured outside of herself, in relation to a man.

Book Resources

- *So Sexy So Soon: The Sexualized Childhood and What Parents Can Do To Protect Their Kids* by Diane E. Levin and Jean Kilbourne
- *Dilemmas of Desire: Teenage Girls Talk About Sexuality* by Deborah Tolman
- *Promiscuities: The Secret Struggle for Womanhood* by Naomi Wolf
- *Slut: Growing Up Female with a Bad Reputation* by Leora Tanenbaum
- *The Purity Myth: How America's Obsession with Virginity is Hurting Young Women* by Jessica Valenti
- *Sex at Dawn: The Prehistoric Origins of Modern Sexuality* by Christopher Ryan and Cacilda Jetha

Online Resources

- Caroline Heldman, the speaker in this video, does an incredible job of explaining the objectification of women, how it's gotten worse, how damaging it is, and what we can do to address it. This video is for women and men: http://www.upworthy.com/being-a-sex-object-is-empowering-oh-wait-no-it-s-not-here-s-why-2

- This is a great article on the prevalence of slut-shaming, called "If You Want a World That Respects Women, Stop Slut-Shaming Them": http://thoughtcatalog.com/nico-lang/2013/08/if-you-want-a-world-that-respects-women-stop-slut-shaming-them/

- This is an amazing blog post from a father to his daughter regarding his wishes for her to have a full and healthy sex life, posted on the *Good Men Project* website, called "I Hope You Have Awesome Sex": http://goodmenproject.com/ethics-values/brand-dear-daughter-i-hope-you-have-awesome-sex/

- Tips to help you with educating your children: http://www.betterhealth.vic.gov.au/bhcv2/bhcarticles.nsf/pages/Sex_education_tips_for_parents

- **SPARK:** SPARK was designed to engage girls as part of the solution rather than to protect them from the problem. A day of workshops and action spots gave girls the tools that they needed to become activists, organizers, researchers, policy influencers, and media makers. For more information, please visit: http://www.sparksummit.com/about-us/

- **Workshops and Camps:** REALgirl Empowerment Programs are unique and innovative programs dedicated to inspiring and guiding girls to discover their *real* (authentic) selves. It is our goal to provide essential life skills that every girl/young woman needs for healthy maturation, development, formation of healthy relationships and for the opportunity to reach her own unique and highest potential. Through art, movement (yoga and dance), discussion, writing, theatre games, guest speakers, and a variety of other dynamic activities, participants will be guided to develop tools to successfully navigate issues that girls face today. To find a camp near you, visit: www.realgirlprograms.com.

CHAPTER 6
WAY #6: LETTING MEDIA SHAPE OUR GIRLS

"The average North American girl will watch 5,000 hours of television, including 80,000 ads, before she starts kindergarten."
—Media Awareness Network, 2010

"You can't be what you can't see."
—Marie Wilson

What We're Doing
In the Western world, by the time the average girl graduates, she will have spent more time engaging with one form of media or another than she will have spent in school. As a child, she is passively programmed by the images and messages that she sees in everything from fairy tales, morning cartoons and "family" movies to billboards and magazine covers. And, with each passing year, she begins to rely more intensively on the media, actively looking for clues for how she is supposed to act as a girl, and some day, as a woman.

In our age of "everywhere media," the messages carried through books, television, movies, magazines, music, and the Internet are constantly shaping a girl's sense of what it means to be female. Make no mistake: most of mainstream media is wreaking havoc on our daughters' self-esteem. Obviously an entire book could be written on this topic alone. For our purposes, I am going to do my very best to cover the key information that we need to know about the messages that our girls receive when we allow them unfiltered access to media.

For many children, books are still the first form of media to which they are exposed. As soon as they are old enough to sit up on our lap, it's our inclination to read stories to them, and those stories almost inevitably include fairy tales. In the chapter on Dad's role, I discussed in some detail the ways in which these stories imprint girls and boys with distinctly different gender roles. The male protagonist is a handsome, rich, charming, brave, problem-solving prince who saves the damsel in distress. The lead female, usually a princess, is passive, submissive, helpless, and naïve, waiting for a prince to save her. Her primary focus is beauty—not intelligence, tenacity, or strength. She forfeits autonomy for dependence in the name of living "happily ever after." The female character who *is* determined, tenacious, and action-oriented is usually the evil witch or stepmother and is trying to do harm to or thwart the princess in some way. Her physical appearance is almost always hideously ugly (think the stepmother in *Snow White*, the evil witch in *Sleeping Beauty*, and Ursula the sea witch in *The Little Mermaid*).

By contrast, the princess is typically illustrated as beautiful, thin, tall, and delicate. Girls quickly learn that emulating the behaviors of the princess make them more "good" and "desirable" while taking charge, being tenacious, and determined are the behaviors of "bad" *and* unattractive females. Girls are left with the feeling that they can *either* be pretty, submissive, and helpless *or* ugly, determined, and action-oriented. The extraordinary power derived when the two exist in combination is wiped off of the map of possibility.

Last, but not least, consistently showing girls that it's other women who will thwart them and a man who will need to save them teaches them to mistrust other women and rely on men to do their problem-solving. This leaves girls disconnected from what could otherwise be extremely important bonds with other females and reliant on someone else (namely men) to save them and bring ultimate happiness to their lives. *These* are the stories, images, and messages that we innocently expose our girls to in their most formative years.

To make matters worse, many of these classic fairy tales have become captivating animated children's or family films that many of us feel safe letting our children watch repeatedly. Dr. Stacy Smith and the Annenberg Foundation, renowned for their work on content patterns pertaining to gender and race, recently released their research findings on a study of 129 top grossing G, PG, and PG-13 films (2006-2011). They determined that less than 30% of all on-screen speaking characters are girls or women, and of those 30%, most are likely to be depicted in a stereotypical (caregivers, romantically involved, lacking employment) and hypersexualized (sexy attire, nudity, thinness) light. In fact, one in four were depicted in sexy, tight, or alluring attire, with exposed skin between the midriff and upper thigh regions, and with waists so small that little room was left for a womb or any other internal organs. Additionally, female characters were far less likely to be depicted in empowered political, business, or legal roles.[1]

When it comes to television, things are not much better. Most of us areot allowing no-holds-barred access, especially when children are little. At the very least, we limit their time in front of the television, and we do our very best to make sure that the language is appropriate for their young ears and that the content is absent of violence that might be traumatizing for their young minds. As long as we stick to the channels and movies dedicated to children, we figure that we're safe. However, as a parent on a mission to raise strong, confident, self-contained girls, I quickly recognized that much of what girls see on children's television shows does not support this goal. Only 30.8% of characters on children's television shows are female and, once again, they are presented in narrowly defined gender roles.[2]

Even on PBS children's shows, which are generally great both because of their educational value and because they are aired without commercials (which are huge culprits in gender stereotyping and programming), only a third of the children's shows currently airing have female main characters and heroes.[2] In cases in which a female "lead" character shares the lead with a male character, the male often holds the trump card. For example, when our daughter was three, my husband "screened" the show *Super Why* for her to watch. He thought it was perfect, because it has a mix of four characters, two males and two females, who work as a team to solve a problem by using their various reading skills. What he missed was that while Princess has the power to spell and Red Riding Hood has the power to rhyme, it's Super Why (Wyatt, when he's not in his superhero form) who is the clear team leader and the only one in the group who has the power to read. Add to this *Sid the Science Kid*, the long running *Arthur*, and Nick Jr.'s *Peter Rabbit* and *PAW Patrol*, and you start to realize that girls are rarely seeing themselves in these shows, and they are certainly not seeing themselves the heroes.

Over and over again, what our daughters see from their earliest years, even through media that we think are safe and educational, is an extremely narrow version of what it means to be female. At best, it generally means being a sidekick to a male hero and, more often than not, a damsel in distress, waiting to be rescued by the male hero. In either case, she had better be ultra-thin and dressed to the nines!

Just as our daughters mimic the way they see us walk and talk, because they watch and interact with us everyday, they also begin to mimic the behavior of and internalize messages about girls and women they receive through television and movies. In one show or movie after the next, day after day, our girls become what they see— and what they see in mainstream media only becomes more overtly disempowering to girls and women as they begin to watch teen and adult programming.

One of the most compelling studies that I've ever seen illustrate this reality examined the impact of television on girls in Fiji. In 1995, television programming was introduced in Fijian homes. At the time, only 5% of girls reported vomiting as a form of weight management. *Just 38 months after TV was introduced*, 15% of girls reported vomiting to control weight, and a staggering 50% of girls who watched television three or more nights per week described themselves as "too fat" compared to non-television watchers.[4]

By 2007, 45% of girls reported purging (vomiting after eating) within the previous month.[5] To put this staggering impact into perspective, it's important to note that Fijian culture embraces full-figured body types for both men and women and "going thin," the expression used when a person loses a noticeable amount of weight, is considered a worrisome condition.[6]

The impact that media have on perceptions of violence against girls and women is also not to be taken lightly. A 2009 study published by the Parents Television Council examined fatal and nonfatal female victimizations as represented on primetime broadcast television from 2004 to 2009. Among their most disturbing findings was a 400%

increase in the depiction of teen girls as victims across all networks. The most frequent type of violence was beating (29%), followed by credible threats of violence (18%), shooting (11%), rape (8%), stabbing (6%), and torture (2%). Among the programs reviewed, violence against women resulted in death 19% of the time. The study ultimately concluded that: *"By depicting violence against women with increasing frequency, or as a trivial, even humorous matter, the networks may be contributing to an atmosphere in which young people view aggression and violence against women as normative, even acceptable."*[7] The very clear message we send to girls when we show them that violence against them is acceptable is this: You don't hold enough value for violence against you to be absolutely *unacceptable*.

What girls are *not* seeing as a regular part of their adolescent viewing experience are female characters who are a combination of smart, strong, professionally successful, capable of creating their own paths, and finding joy within themselves (rather than having to be completed by a man). We reserve this powerful blend of qualities almost exclusively for male characters. The airwaves continue to be almost completely absent of women who are leaders of corporations or presidents of their country. So what does all this have to do with girls developing low self-esteem? As the brilliant and important documentary *Miss Representation* reminds us, we cannot *be* what we cannot *see*. Until the media broadens its currently narrow depictions of what it means to be female—less powerful than men, not capable of leading, damsels in distress whose mission in life it is to find a man— the possibilities that most girls envision for themselves will continue to be equally narrow.

And it gets worse. By the time girls move into their tween years, another especially detrimental form of media starts to peak their interest—teen magazines. Eighty-three percent of teenage girls surveyed reported reading fashion magazines for about 4.3 hours each week.[8] Teen magazines, filled with digitally enhanced images of underweight models, impossibly perfect skin, and an endless array of product advertisements (promising to make her more popular, beautiful, and happy) become a trusted source of guidance for adolescent girls. Studies done with girls from ages twelve to fifteen concluded that girls look to these magazines as much as they do to their friends for fashion and beauty advice.[9] In-depth interviews with girls ages twelve and thirteen also determined that the girls used these magazines to formulate their concepts of femininity *and* that they rely heavily on articles that feature boys' opinions about how to gain male approval.[10]

In preparation for a workshop that I was facilitating, I randomly picked up a copy of *Seventeen*, hoping to find a couple of solid examples of negative messages for girls. Little did I know that it would contain examples on virtually every page. In one of the magazine's major features, girls are given tips on how to "change your body." These include how to use clothing and accessories to "look taller," "play up your bust," "trim your middle," and make "your booty pop."[11]

In another four-page spread, girls are provided with tips for behavior in relation to boys. Titled "50 Ways to be a Better Flirt," here are the tips that they find:

> *#14: **Ask him out "by accident."** Text him "What r u up to tonite?" When he replies, say "Sorry, that was for a friend—but yeah, what r u doing?" The tiny diss will make him work harder.*
>
> *#26: **Paint your nails a super-girly color.** It will help you get in touch with your flirty side—and make you think about how great your hands will look playfully wrapped around the bicep of a cutie.*
>
> *#37: **Leave him wanting more.** Go in for a kiss at the end of the night—but then turn your head and whisper you had a nice time instead!*
>
> *#50: **Don't discuss hooking up.** Steering your conversations in that direction makes it seem like sex is all you're interested in—and most guys are freaked out by that kind of aggression.*[12]

In relation to boys and men, girls are rarely encouraged in these magazines to be connected to their own interests and desires and in charge of communicating what they want. Rather, as the "tips" above illustrate, she is not to make a boy uncomfortable with her aggression and she should essentially be sexy without being overtly sexual. Just being herself and trusting her instincts in the moment are completely ignored. Nowhere in the extensive number of teen magazines that I researched were there clear, encouraging messages to girls that they always have the right to say "no" and that they should expect their "no" to be adhered to.

Part of what makes fashion and teen magazines so alluring is that they are marketed as a source for helping the reader "better" herself. In reality, the messages that our daughters absorb from these magazines have nothing to do with inspiring them to be strong, confident, self-reliant girls. Instead, they act as formidable tools that program girls to believe that their power lies exclusively in their physical beauty and their ability to be attractive to the opposite sex. Studies have shown that frequent magazine reading was consistently correlated with higher levels of body dissatisfaction and disordered eating,[13] and even brief interaction resulted in feelings of depression, stress, guilt, shame, and insecurity.[14] Our girls start down what can be a lifelong struggle to meet an impossible, literally unreal standard of physical beauty, and the consequence of this can be dire. By the age of thirteen, approximately 53% of American girls are "unhappy with their bodies," and this number will increase to 78% by the time girls reach seventeen years of age.[15] Even grown women, after brief exposure to just eleven media images of females, reported increased levels of body dissatisfaction and weight anxiety.[16] We really shouldn't expect anything different when the resounding and consistent message they get is *"You're not good enough!"*

The media's not going away. Nor do we want it to. I'm not suggesting that we cut our daughters off from it entirely. But, I am suggesting that we start being diligent about our own media literacy, and that of our children, so that the almost inevitable cultural programming and detrimental effects of television, movies, and magazines do not go unchallenged. As consumers, we have tremendous power to dictate what is "aired" and published. Unfortunately, most of us simply do not have the time to fight that battle. At the very least, what we must *make* the time to do, if we hope to protect our daughters from one of the most pervasive sources of disempowering messages to our girls, is filter and monitor what she is allowed to read and view when she is young, and ensure that her media literacy skills and her own media filter become really strong as she grows older. Her overall health and wellbeing, not to mention her ability to reach her highest potential, may depend on it.

How We Can Stop

1. **Develop and give the gift of media literacy.** Studies have shown that girls and women who are less aware of the media's effects are much more likely to show symptoms of negative body image issues.[17] Becoming media-literate, first for ourselves and then as effective guides to our children, is essential to fighting the battle to protect girls' self-esteem. Media literacy involves understanding the influence behind the media and the source of its power. More than anything, the media is controlled by money. The shows that air on television and the content that goes into magazines are primarily determined by advertising, and the goal of advertisers is to get us to keep consuming. The most effective way to get people in the Western world to buy is to convince us that something is wrong with us and then offer a solution that we can purchase. Once we recognize this, we can start looking at all media through a filter that catches these messages and sees them for what they are. Instead of penetrating our brains (and our children's brains) and shaping the way that we feel about ourselves, they become annoyingly insulting to our intelligence. This is one of the most empowering tools that we can give our kids.

2. **Become an expert at spotting gender stereotyping.** Your media literacy filter will also be critical for recognizing gender stereotypes that are everywhere in mainstream media. I strongly recommend screening the books, television shows, and movies that your kids are going to engage with before they do. While they are really young, taking the time to do so will set a strong precedent. When you do, ask these questions:
   - Is this the old "damsel in distress who gets rescued by the knight/prince story again?" *(Once you become aware, these are especially easy to spot in children's stories, family movies, and romantic comedies.)*
   - Is there a strong lead female character?
   - Are the supporting female characters portrayed as strong and independent?

- Do the female characters exhibit qualities and behaviors that I want my daughter to aspire to?
- Are they treated respectfully by their male counterparts?
- Are they valued for what they can do rather than just the way that they look?
- Does the story demonstrate equality and partnership between the male and female characters?

If you're answering "no" to these questions, move on to another option. When this is not possible, create a teachable moment by talking through these questions with your kids before and after to heighten their awareness.

3. **Choose wisely when it comes to bedtime stories.** Thankfully, there are increasingly more stories being written and fairy tales being *re-written* with female characters that are so much more than just damsels in distress. One of my all-time favorites is Robert Munsch's *The Paper Bag Princess*, in which a dragon carries off Prince Ronald to his lair and Princess Elizabeth, with great courage and wit, saves Ronald. When he tells her that she doesn't look like a princess in her paper bag, she basically tells him to take a hike and doesn't marry him after all! Stories like these, whether in book or movie form, are essential to putting an end to the message that a girl's or a woman's value is defined by her relationship to a man.

4. **Limit TV time.** Studies have found that women who reported greater exposure to television programming during adolescence were more likely to experience negative body image issues.[18] This, coupled with the many other negative outcomes associated with excessive television viewing such as obesity, desensitization to violence, and impaired academic performance, is strong motivation for us to do the not-so-pleasant task of limiting and monitoring both content *and* quantity.[10] With my older daughter, our objective was to avoid commercials whenever possible, and to provide as many shows with strong female characters. To that end,

we limited her to DVD series like *Buffy, Xena,* and *Veronica Mars.* Anything else that she watched on regular television we tried to watch together, so that we could be aware and actively involved in filtering. If it's any consolation, I didn't know what I know now, until she was about five years old. Even starting our media diligence at that point has made an enormous difference in her overall self-perception as a girl, her confidence, and many of her behaviors.

With my younger daughter, there is more access to programs that are mostly commercial-free (although they sneak them in at the end between shows), so we tape those and allow her to watch about an hour per day on school days and slightly more on the weekend. The American Academy of Pediatrics discourages all screen-based media exposure for children under the age of two and recommends no more than two hours daily for kids over the age of two. This includes video games, movies, and Internet, both on the phone and the computer.[20] Believe me, I know how challenging this can be with the insane schedules so many of us attempt to maintain. The trick is to start this as early as possible. Avoid putting television sets in your child's bedroom (where it's much more difficult to monitor), and try to be consistent with your own viewing habits, at least while the kids are awake.

For more great tips to help you get creative with limiting TV time, please check out this great article from the Mayo Clinic: http://www.mayoclinic.org/children-and-tv/art-20047952?pg=2

5. **Establish a *Fashion Magazine-Free Zone.*** As I've illustrated in detail, the damage that these magazines do to girls' self-image and self-esteem cannot be overstated. Spare yourself and your daughter the torture of being told on page after page that the current way that you look is simply not good enough. Nothing that they're selling will make you look like the digitally enhanced models on those pages anyway. If your daughter is already well into adolescence and would be highly resistant to this, take the time to explain why. You may

even want to introduce her to the efforts of other girls who are taking on fashion magazines because of their detrimental effects on girls and women. In 2012, fourteen-year-old Julia Bluhm successfully petitioned *Seventeen* Magazine to portray girls more truthfully (i.e. without digital manipulation). Sometimes knowing that they can actually do something to change a reality that is harmful is just the nudge girls need to feel empowered and take action. You can find information about Julia and her efforts here: http://www.huffingtonpost.com/2012/07/05/julia-bluhm-seventeen-mag_n_1650938.html

6. **Find the gems.** Thanks to great documentary films like *Killing Us Softly* and *Miss Representation,* we have become increasingly aware of the connection between media messages and low self-value among girls and women. Consequently, increasing efforts are being made to create pro-girl or girl-healthy magazines, books, shows, and movies. Disney-Pixar's *Brave* was a *huge* leap forward for girls, because it turned upside down so many traditional norms that keep girls in narrowly defined and limiting gender roles. Most of the time, these gems are just a little harder to find than all the others. I have included a link to a great new collection of books and movies for parents who are "dedicated to raising smart, confident and courageous girls." It's called *A Mighty Girl* (www.amightygirl.com).

7. **Bring other moms on board.** Whether you do so by inviting a group of moms of girls over for a screening of *Killing Us Softly* or *Miss Representation* or you work to spread the word by sharing your media literacy mission over coffee, email, social networking, or whatever, bringing other moms on board will grow your efforts exponentially and make your media mission with your daughter that much easier. I've seen moms express concern that if they restrict their daughter's media consumption, this might ostracize her in some way within her circle of friends. First, I'm not a fan of parenting in

fear. Second, if her friends are hearing the same message from their moms, you won't have a problem. You also won't have to worry about what she's being exposed to at play dates and sleepovers if everyone is on the same page!

Resources

Documentaries/Videos That Will Help to Teach Media Literacy

- *Miss Representation*
- *Killing Us Softly*
- *Dove Evolution Videos*

Books for Parents

- *Cinderella Ate My Daughter: Dispatches From the Front Lines of the New Girlie-Girl Culture* by Peggy Orenstein
- *So Sexy So Soon* by Jean Kilbourne and Diane Levin
- *Can't Buy My Love* by Jean Kilbourne

Online Resources for Parents

- *Common Sense Media:* Common Sense Media is dedicated to improving the lives of kids and families by providing the trustworthy information, education, and independent voice that they need to thrive in a world of media and technology. As a non-partisan, not-for-profit organization, they provide trustworthy information and tools, as well as an independent forum, so that families can have a choice and a voice about the media that they consume *(http://www.commonsensemedia. org/about-us/our-mission).*
- *A Mighty Girl*—the world's largest collection of books, toys and movies for smart, confident, and courageous girls *(www. amightygirl.com)*

Girl-Friendly Films and Shows
- *Brave*
- *Muan*

Girl-Friendly Books (some of my favorites)
From birth through age seven
- *The Paper Bag Princess* by Robert Munsch
- *Rosie Reveer, Engineer* by Andrea Beaty and David Roberts
- *The Watcher* by Jeanette Winter
- *Willow* by Denise Brennan-Nelson, Rosemarie Brennan and Cyd Moore

For ages eight through eleven
- *New Moon Magazine*
- *Girls Rule* by Ashley Rice
- *Real Beauty: 101 Ways to Feel Great About YOU (American Girl)* by Therese Kauchak
- *Real Spirit: Fun Ideas for Refreshing, Relaxing, and Staying Strong (American Girl)* by Elizabeth Chobanian
- *The Care & Keeping of YOU Journal (American Girl)* by Norm Bendell
- *A Smart Girl's Guide to Friendship Troubles (American Girl)* by Patti Kelley Criswell

For ages twelve through seventeen
- *I am an Emotional Creature* by Eve Ensler (for girls and parents)
- *The Goddess In Every Girl: Develop Your Teen Feminine Power* by M.J. Abadie
- *The Thundering Years: Rituals and Sacred Wisdom for Teens* by Julie Tallard Johnson
- *1001 Things Everyone Should Know About Women's History* by Constance Jones

Online Resources for Girls

- *New Moon Girls* is an inspirational magazine and online site for girls age eight and up to engage in self-discovery, creativity, and community (http://www.newmoon.com/).

- *Miss O and Friends* was started in 2005 by a teenager named Juliette Brindak, and uses a multicultural group of real-life friends as muses and inspiration for its offerings, which encourage creativity, curiosity, and a positive outlook on life. This site is very positively rated by commonsensemedia.org (http://www.missoandfriends.com/).

- *SPARK* is designed to engage girls as part of the solution, rather than to protect them from the problem. A terrific place for girls to blog and be involved with other girls advocating for themselves with media and societal messages that demean and disempower girls (http://www.sparksummit.com/)

CHAPTER 7
WAY #7: PASSING ON PATRIARCHY IN OUR SCHOOLS

"Women and men continue to replay behaviors they learned as children at school, and teachers continue to teach the way they were taught."
—Karen R. Zittleman, *Still Failing at Fairness*

"When those who have the power to name and to socially construct reality choose not to see you or hear you ... when someone with the authority of a teacher, say, describes the world and you are not in it, there is a moment of psychic disequilibrium, as if you looked in the mirror and saw nothing. It takes some strength of soul—and not just individual strength, but collective understanding—to resist this void, this non-being, into which you are thrust, and to stand up, demanding to be seen and heard."
—Adrienne Rich

What We're Doing

First, I need to acknowledge the phenomenal dedication that so many teachers bring to the classroom every day. Having taught in public middle and high school classrooms for a decade, I know firsthand the many, varied, and often frustrating limitations that teachers face on a daily basis. Most do their very best with what they have. That said, my experience on the inside also gave me a bird's-eye view of the many shortcomings of "traditional" schools that are not being addressed because the whole system is so stuck in the *status quo*.

This chapter is dedicated to shedding light on this important realm of our children's lives, so that we may look closely at the way in which it is perpetuating gender inequities, and make it better for all.

When we enroll our children in school, we make the tremendous leap of faith, just as our parents did, that they will be guided and inspired toward their own unique version of greatness. Our daughters and our sons enter an environment that they have been told is an authority on the world. Their filters are off and they trust both the curriculum and messages taught within the classroom environment to be true. As a result, this is a particularly potent realm of their lives when it comes to developing their perceptions of the world *and* their place within it. Unfortunately, what both girls and boys typically learn is that the role of women in the construction of our society has been less prevalent and less valuable then that of men.

In 1995, the American Association of University Women published a report called *How Schools Are Shortchanging Our Girls.* The groundbreaking report explored gender as it applied to the classroom environment (including teaching methods) and the curriculum itself. It also examined the difference in the self-esteem of boys and girls in early and later school years as a measure of the effectiveness of the nation's public-school system. The study found that while "girls and boys enter school roughly equal in measured ability, twelve years later, girls have fallen behind their male classmates in key areas such as higher-level mathematics and measures of self-esteem." Unfortunately, although it was written two decades ago, the most recent research on gender equity in classrooms suggests that very little has changed.[1]

First let's look at the messages that are taught in the classroom environment. According to gender equity specialists Myra and David Sadker, teachers frequently interact differently with boys than they do with girls—and this plays an important role in shaping self-esteem for both. After observing one hundred classrooms in four different states, the Sadkers determined that boys benefited greatly from the opportunity to enhance self-esteem because they overwhelmingly dominate the proceedings, consistently command more of the teacher's time and energy than girls, and consequently receive more positive reinforcement, remediation, and criticism.[2]

As a result of her own extensive classroom observations, *Schoolgirls* author Peggy Orenstein concurred that this kind of interaction is critical to the development of self-esteem:

> *Speaking out in class—and being acknowledged for it—is a constant reinforcement of a student's right to be heard, to take academic risks. Students who talk in class have more opportunity to enhance self-esteem through exposure to praise; they have the luxury of learning from mistakes and they develop the perspective to see failure as an educational tool... The important thing is to be recognized, to assert the "I am."*[3]

The Sadkers also concluded that "boys...were commended for their academic acumen, while girls were commended for social skills and docility."[4]

My own team recently conducted a survey with 150 girls and boys in the sixth, seventh, and eighth grades, the results of which clearly echoed these findings. The overwhelming majority of girls (94%) *and* boys (87%) stated that, more often than not, boys shout out answers in class. One sixth-grade girl commented that "Sometimes girls have their hands up for like thirty minutes and boys just shout out the answer." A seventh-grade girl commented, "Boys shout out and the teacher doesn't care, but when a girl does, she gets in trouble." One sixth-grade boy stated that boys yell out answers in class while girls sit with their hands up, "because we are more confident."[5] Clearly, teachers come in with their own sense of "normal," "expected" or "acceptable" behaviors from each gender and this translates in their classroom management and interactions.

Certainly boys should not be faulted for their vigor in the classroom. But clearly there is a need for teachers to be aware of these findings and a need for their commitment to encourage the active participation of girls as well as boys. Showing unmistakable value for the contributions, successes, *and* tenacity of girls is essential to their development of personal agency and self-efficacy. From the earliest grades onward, teachers must be conscious and diligent in doing so. It's also important that boys *see* these qualities being valued in girls.

A study done in the 1980s illustrated this point very poignantly. The study, conducted by psychologist Carol Dweck, looked at how bright girls and bright boys in the fifth grade handled new, difficult, and confusing material. When bright and even straight-A girls were given something new to learn, especially if it was foreign or complex, they were quick to give up and showed helpless responses. Bright boys, however, saw the difficult material as a challenge and found it energizing.[6] Dweck determined that this had nothing to do with the innate ability of either the girls or the boys. In fact, fifth-grade girls consistently outperform boys in every subject, including math and science. The only difference was how the bright girls and bright boys *interpreted* difficulty: "Bright girls were much quicker to *doubt* their ability, to lose confidence, and to become less effective learners as a result...they believe that their abilities are innate and unchangeable, while bright boys believe that they can develop ability through effort and practice."[7]

The primary reason for this difference? Girls are consistently praised for their "goodness" and their "self-control." Whereas boys, who tend to be more active and demonstrate less self-control, are constantly told that if they'd just pay attention they'd learn, or that if they'd just try a little harder they could get it right. The study concluded that, because boys are given a lot more feedback that specifically emphasizes effort, when they face something difficult their default is not to internalize the difficulty as a sign of their innate inability but, rather, to see it as a sign that they need to try harder.[8]

It's also important to note this study as clear evidence that boys are successfully being socialized to view themselves as active participants in their own world. Having personal agency becomes part of their constitution, so putting forth effort makes sense. Combine this with the many examples they see of other males successfully reaching goals and shaping their environment and they believe in their own ability to do the same (self-efficacy). In contrast, the default behaviors of bright girls make it evident that we are not doing the same for them. Girls question both their personal agency and self-efficacy because we are not facilitating the development of these important "internal muscles," as I like to call them. With each passing year of socialization, they see themselves not as valuable and effective architects of their environment, but as passive recipients of feedback that has the power to define their ability and social worth. (In fairness, school is not the only culprit when it comes to this aspect of girls' socialization.) This programming stays with them well beyond the school years and these girls become women who doubt their ability to succeed in any number of areas of life and end up not bothering to try. Their willingness to "lean in," as Sheryl Sanberg so aptly put it, and seize opportunities to contribute their voice, talent, and potential becomes significantly diminished and we all end up functioning at a deficit.

When girls are not encouraged to be active, tenacious participants whose contributions are valued in the earlier grades (both in school and other realms of their lives), by the latter part of middle school, teachers end up facing the challenge of getting girls to participate at all. Spontaneous sharing of answers during middle- and high-school classroom lessons is usually the most difficult arena in which to get girls to speak up. The reasons that girls give for *why* they're not participating are very telling:

- *"I don't raise my hand in my classes because I'm afraid I have the wrong answer and I'll be embarrassed. My self-confidence will be taken away..."*
- *"I think girls just worry about what people will say more than boys do, so they don't want to talk so much."*
- *"Boys never care if they're wrong. They can say totally off-the-wall things, things that have nothing to do with class sometimes. They're not afraid to get in trouble or anything. I'm not shy. But it's like, when I get into class, I just... I just can't talk. I don't know why."*[9]

On the other hand, one of the boys from the same eighth-grade group made this very telling statement:

> *I think my opinions are important, so I yell them out. The teacher'll tell you not to do it, but they answer your question before the people who raise their hands. Girls will sit there until the bell rings with their hands up and never get their question answered. Forget that.*[10]

Once again, our own survey results yielded almost identical responses. When asked if they were sometimes afraid to answer a question in class for fear of being wrong, 84% of sixth-grade girls and 79% of seventh-grade girls said "yes." Two eighth-grade girls also commented that they were afraid of being wrong because "the boys [would] laugh" at them. A seventh-grade girl commented, "Yes, because I feel like, what if I get it really wrong and people think I'm dumb?" By contrast, only 10% of sixth-grade boys and 24% of seventh-grade boys answered "yes" to the same question. One seventh-grade boy commented, "No way, boys never have that fear."[11] These painful insecurities in academic settings can and often do compromise the ability of girls to get the most out of their education, which should be one of their greatest sources of empowerment.

Now let's look at how the curriculum itself further shapes girls' sense of their place and value in the world. Textbooks are still the most widely used means of providing curricula in schools, with the average teacher using them for seventy to ninety percent of the classroom time.[12] They are particularly potent in their influence because most students view them as the official, authoritative version of the world, even when their content bores them to tears.

Across the board of core subjects, the contributions and experiences of women are marginalized or ignored in many textbooks. This happened, in part, because until women were allowed to be formally educated in our colleges, their opportunity to participate in recording our history in books was almost non-existent (hence "*his*tory"). To put this into perspective, imagine for a moment that your family decided to start recording its historical highlights and accomplishments for future generations—but only the men would write it. Think about all the experiences, memories, and milestones that would be lost and how incomplete the picture of your family's history would be. Unfortunately, those reading it in the future, unless encouraged to see the "holes," would just assume that what they were reading was actually a complete history. This has been the reality of the bulk of our recorded history across various disciplines until very recently.

History textbooks are the most obvious culprits when it comes to lacking gender parity. Various studies show that the representation of women in history textbooks has been extremely lacking. In the 1970s, only 5.9 females were mentioned for every 100 males mentioned, and by the 1990s it had increased to a mere 10.6 females for every 100 males.[13] Women's valuable roles in raising families and building and sustaining communities, as well as their contributions to science, innovation, and politics have all been overshadowed by the accomplishments of men. In our survey with middle-school students, we asked if women were presented in their classroom as strong, valuable contributors to our history and present society. An eighth-grade girl responded, "We haven't learned about women's history yet."[14] In high-school English classes across the nation, the ten most commonly used works of literature include: *The Adventures of Huck Finn, The Scarlet Letter, To Kill a Mockingbird, The Red Badge of Courage, The Great Gatsby, The Grapes of Wrath, Call of the Wild, Invisible Man: A Novel, A Farewell to Arms,* and *Fahrenheit 451*. Only one of these classic novels—*To Kill a Mockingbird*—was authored by a female, Harper Lee, whom many don't realize is female. Not coincidentally, it's also the only novel with a memorably strong female main character. Imagine the very different impact if teachers highlighted the reality that great female writers of the past had to write under male pen names in order to be taken seriously. Imagine the impact if students knew that even Joanne Rowling, the staggeringly successful author of the *Harry Potter* series, was advised in 1997 to take on the pen name "J.K. Rowling" for fear that boys would not read her books if they knew that they were written by a woman. It is essential that teachers creatively and constructively use their knowledge and authority to point out what is wrong with this reality, and to encourage students to think differently.

Science textbooks have also been found to have minimal information regarding the many accomplishments of women in science.[15] Women are underrepresented in both text and in images, with only one of the seven most commonly used science textbooks reviewed showing equal images of both men and women.[16] Worse yet, when women were pictured, they were usually shown in positions inferior to men and as passive actors merely reacting to their surroundings, while men were shown as active in altering the situation around them.[17] The message to the students using these seemingly infallible textbooks is that women are either absent in the meaningful construction of our world or involved in roles that are inferior to those of men. It would be absurd to think that this doesn't have a deep and disparaging impact on the way girls *and boys* perceive the value and contribution of females in our society.

Researchers believe that these stereotypical images and messages contribute to girls' perceptions that boys are simply better at science and math, and this ultimately impacts their academic performance.[18] One study looked at the impact of illustrations in chemistry textbooks on girls' academic performance. Ninth-grade students were divided into three groups and given identical content pages with one key difference. One third had pages that included illustrations of men only, one third were given pages with pictures of women only, and the final third included pictures of both male and female chemists. The girls who read exactly the same material but saw illustrations in textbooks of exclusively female scientists demonstrated "significantly higher comprehension of the science lesson" than girls in the groups with all-male images or mixed male and female images.[19] The fact that an analysis of eighty science textbooks from both elementary and secondary schools concluded that eighty-five percent of the occupations pictured were embodied by men does not bode well for our girls.[20] This may explain why girls at age nine still desire to participate in science-based activities, but by the age of thirteen, report significantly less desire for such experiences. They are essentially being "taught" which academic pursuits are appropriate for them and which are not.

This has very real and tangible consequences for their future, too. In 2013 the seven highest-paying master's degrees all involved math-and/or science-based knowledge.[21] If girls don't see themselves as having a place in the realm of math and science, they are put at a disadvantage economically. The ability of our girls, as future women, to have the greatest number of occupational options, and to provide for themselves financially, is a critical piece of their empowerment. Women who are capable of providing for themselves and contributing to the financial "pot" as co-breadwinners are much less vulnerable to becoming stuck in unhealthy relationships. They are also better able to deal with divorce or even the death of their spouse when they are able to create some financial security of their own. Unfortunately, the number of women in these fields will continue to suffer for as long as our girls remain limited by the gender stereotypes being reinforced at school. At the end of the day, this has implications for us all because we are underutilizing the tremendous resources that the female half of our population would bring to the table if they believed there was a place for them.

On a positive note, the implementation of STEM (Science Technology Engineering Math) programs for girls throughout the nation are yielding great results. Girls who have participated in programs like Operation SMART, Science Club for Girls (SCFG), and Tech Bridge are expressing a shift in the way that they feel about their knowledge, ability, and valuable role in STEM fields. This has direct benefits for girls in terms of expanding their future horizons in STEM but, in our broader reality, these results also demonstrate the change that is possible when a concerted effort is made to improve education standards and opportunities.[22]

In the meantime, the use of textbooks lacking in gender parity will most certainly continue to shape the perceptions girls and boys develop about both gender roles and the value that men and women hold within our society. The absence and misrepresentation of women in these texts leads to the reasonable conclusion by readers that women have made few contributions to culture, play a less significant role, and therefore hold less value than men in shaping our society. Ironically, the books that are meant to be vehicles for learning are, in many cases, actually hindering the success of half of the student population.

In the 1970s two important laws promised to make a difference in the lives of girls and women by requiring schools and institutions of higher learning to advance gender equity. Title IX, with which most people are familiar, is a civil rights law that prohibits sex-based discrimination against both students and employees in federally funded education programs and activities. It is a great example of how significant and how impactful change can be for girls and women in various parts of their lives, including access to higher education, athletics, employment, the reduction of sexual harassment, and more.

This chart shows the great distance that we have covered and the territory that is in jeopardy of being lost or has yet to be known:

	Before Title IX	After Title IX
Access to Higher Education	• Many colleges and universities set quotas limiting women's admission and subjected women to tougher admissions criteria. • Female applicants to doctoral programs often had to explain how they would combine a career with family. • Schools gave preference to men in the awarding of scholarships, fellowships, and loans.	• Many financial aid programs have been modified to facilitate women's access to higher education. • Women earn more than half of the associate's, bachelor's, and master's degrees, but still lag behind men at the doctoral level, earning just thirty-nine percent of doctoral degrees. • Women are still underrepresented in math and science, fields that have been hostile to women.

Source: National Coalition for Women and Girls in Education,
http://www.ncwge.org/PDF/TitleIXat25-summary.pdf

In Athletics	• Girls were just 1% of all high-school athletes. Fewer than 32,000 women competed in intercollegiate athletics. • Athletic scholarships for women were virtually nonexistent. • Athletic opportunities for female students frequently were limited to cheerleading. • Female college athletes received only 2% of overall athletic budgets.	• Girls account for 40% of all high school athletes. Women are 37%of all college varsity athletes. • Female athletes receive only 23% of athletic scholarship dollars, 38% of athletic scholarship dollars, and 27% of athletic recruiting dollars. • The number of female coaches in college athletics has decreased, down to 48%from 90% in the 1970s.

Source: National Coalition for Women and Girls in Education,
http://www.ncwge.org/PDF/TitleIXat25-summary.pdf

Career Education	• High schools were typically segregated vocational education classes by sex: girls took home economics, and boys took shop.	• Men remain clustered in high-skill, high-wage job tracks, while women predominate in low-wage, traditionally female tracks, even in new School-to-Work programs.
	• At the postsecondary level, women trained for low-wage, traditionally female jobs in health and cosmetology; men trained for jobs in trade and industry and technical occupations.	• Congress is poised to repeal state requirements that successfully have helped women, particularly displaced homemakers and single parents, gain access to non-traditional occupations.
	• Certain vocational schools, such as automotive and aviation schools, were reserved for men.	

Source: National Coalition for Women and Girls in Education,
http://www.ncwge.org/PDF/TitleIXat25-summary.pdf

The second big gender equity law was the Women's Educational Equity Act of 1974 (WEEA). WEEA is a subpart of Title V of the Elementary and Secondary Education Act, and its primary objectives are to promote gender equity in education in the United States, and to promote equity in education for girls and women who suffer from multiple forms of discrimination based on sex, race, origin, limited English proficiency, disability or age. It is also charged with the important job of providing financial assistance to enable educational agencies and institutions to meet the requirements of Title IX. This includes providing training in gender equity for teachers and other school personnel, so it is clearly of the utmost importance.

Unfortunately, WEEA has seldom been granted enough funds to fulfill its important mission, a fact that speaks volumes about the true value placed on gender equity in this country's educational institutions. Although it was authorized for $80 million in 1980, only $10 million was received that year, the most it has ever received to date. On average, it has been granted about $4 million per year. In 2003, the Bush Administration officially closed the WEEA Equity Resource Center, which reduced much of the program's capacity to be effective. Since 2010, the Department of Education has not funded any WEEA program grants and in 2014 the President's budget does not request funds for WEEA.[23]

Of course, this is deeply disappointing. Education *should* equal empowerment. But that hinges significantly on the quality and comprehensiveness of the knowledge that a student collects about the world and the value of her or his place in it. In this extraordinarily important realm of girls' lives, they must experience the value of their own voices, learn the benefit of trial and error, and witness abundant examples of women who have come before them. By the same token, boys need to know they have partners in the construction of our world, as did all the men who came before *them*.

This is currently not the case, but we are not helpless. Whether you are paying for your child's education with taxes or tuition, your dollars *and your votes* hold the power to affect change. An overhaul of teacher training and textbooks is an essential and powerful starting place. And if our schools, primed to help shape the minds of the future, can get it right, there is great hope for our larger society.

How We Can Stop

1. **Heighten your own awareness.** As always, start with your own crash course on gender-fair curricula and classrooms. Hopefully this chapter serves as a strong foundation to build upon with some of the resources that I list below. As your awareness heightens, many of the other action steps will take shape organically.

2. **If you have a choice, choose wisely.** Whether preparing for preschool or the K-12 academic journey, if you have a choice about what school your daughter will attend, make your assessment with a whole new set of criteria. Be aware of how school environments and curricula shape your daughter's self-value and make a list of strong questions. Interview school admissions directors and counselors to determine their level of commitment to a gender-balanced curriculum. You can assess how "girl-conscious" their school environment is from teacher's attitudes, gender equity awareness, and the school curriculum, including textbooks. It's all equally important! Here are three basic questions that you can ask:

    • *Have your teachers gone through some sort of gender-equity training?*

    • *Were the textbooks purchased for use in classrooms chosen with gender parity in mind?*

    • *Do your English Language Arts teachers make a conscious effort to utilize works of literature that have female protagonists and strong female characters, at least fifty percent of the time?*

3. **Get involved.** Regardless of whether you are paying for your child's school through taxes or tuition, as a parent you have the right, the opportunity, and the obligation to be as involved as your time and energy allow you to be. This may be as minimal as perusing her schoolbooks and homework assignments and having daily conversations around the dinner table to hear about what she learned at school. Or it may be more involved, through volunteering in her classroom or becoming part of

the PTA. Your awareness of what she is learning in school and how it is shaping her sense of her self as a girl is a critical part of ensuring that she is guided to reach her highest potential.

4. **Request speakers on this subject.** Schools often bring in speakers to present on various subjects that they think parents will be interested in hearing about. Find out who's in charge of booking speakers in your school or district and make a request for a speaker on the subject of gender equity in schools. You might have an even greater chance at success if you do the research to find someone first, and then just send over the contact information and bio to the person responsible for doing the booking. The added benefit of this is that, as more parents become aware of how detrimental it is to girls *and* boys to maintain the patriarchal *status quo* in schools, the sooner we will see a collective shift.

5. **Encourage your daughter to use her voice.** While you may have limited control as parents over what goes on inside your daughter's classroom from one day to the next, you do have a significant amount of control over the knowledge that she already has under her belt when she leaves the house. The more time and effort you spend at home creating a reality where girls and women have valued perspectives and opinions, the more likely your daughter is to notice when this is missing. Encourage her to speak up when she witnesses inequality in her school curricula and environment, and support her when she does.

Book Resources
- *SchoolGirls: Young Women, Self-Esteem, and the Confidence Gap* by Peggy Orenstein
- *Still Failing at Fairness: How Gender Bias Cheats Girls and Boys in School and What We Can Do About It* by David & Myra Sadker and Karen R. Zittleman
- *1001 Things Everyone Should Know About Women's History* by Constance Jones

Online Resources

- US Department of Education (Women's Educational Equity Act): http://www2.ed.gov/policy/elsec/leg/esea02/pg86.html
- Creating Gender Equity in Your Teaching: http://wrrc.ucdavis.edu/files/misc/genderequity.pdf

CHAPTER 8
WAY #8: RAISING "PLEASERS"

"I think the act of pleasing makes everything murky. We lose track of ourselves. We stop uttering declaratory sentences. We stop directing our lives… We forget what we know. We make everything okay rather than real."

—Eve Ensler

"I can't tell you the key to success, but the key to failure is trying to please everyone."

—Ed Sheeran

What We're Doing

My five-year-old doesn't hesitate to tell me that she's emphatically *not* wearing a dress because it's difficult to play in. Nor does she think twice about passionately protesting to her teacher the school rule that restricts kindergarteners from playing on the monkey bars and demanding to know why. These may sound inconsequential to an adult, but they are extremely meaningful in her world. She is speaking her mind and, in the case of the dress, outright refusing something that may literally limit her ability to move freely in the world. Her inclination is not to compromise her own needs in order to please me, nor is it to please her teacher. She believes that her desire to play without being restricted by a dress and her dissatisfaction with a rule that prevents her from playing on the monkey bars are valuable and worth expressing. She believes that *she* is valuable and worthy of having a voice.

This is the way most girls come into the world—connected to themselves, in charge, and unapologetic for their own thoughts, feelings, and desires. As Patricia Lynn Reilly so beautifully summarizes in *Imagine a Woman in Love with Herself*:

> *In the very beginning, the girl-child loves herself. She comes into the world with feelings of omnipotence, not inferiority. She loves her body, expresses its needs, and follows its impulses. She recognizes and expresses her feelings. She tells the truth. She is interested in herself and enjoys private time. She is involved with herself and her own pursuits. She celebrates herself and expects acknowledgment for her creativity and accomplishments. She does not expend one ounce of her precious life-energy trying to figure out what is wrong with her body, feelings, and thoughts. She just lives.*[1]

Sadly, by the time girls approach adolescence, this reality will have shifted dramatically. A staggering 74% of girls between third and twelfth grade say that they are under pressure to please everyone.[2] The need to please applies to various aspects of their being and behavior, including their physical appearance (physical "perfection," dressing "right," being thin), as well as needing to speak softly, not brag, and play caretaker roles. Every day, girls expend an extraordinary amount of precious energy trying to figure out what they need to say, do, and change about themselves in order to please others. Instead of adolescence being a time of deeper self-discovery and identity formation, for girls it often becomes the opposite. In the process of trying to become what everyone else tells them that they need to be, they become disconnected from their sense of identity, their passions, and their unique personal desires. As Jane Fonda put it, it's like they move out of themselves and move in next door.[3]

Why do girls do this? Because we, as a society, tell them that they must do so in order to be acceptable, desirable, successful women. We constantly reinforce with our gender norms that feminine behavior involves a self-sacrificing brand of nurturing others and engagement in non-threatening, accommodating, and even submissive interactions. Understanding how we are usually unknowingly guiding her down the path to "Pleaserdom" as parents is essential to changing our behavior and helping her to stay whole.

To be clear, I am not suggesting that girls shouldn't be encouraged to be kind and caring toward others. The innate ability and desire to nurture, with which most girls and women arrive on the planet, is not to be underestimated in its value or power. Whether through the nurturing of children or the capacity to create world-changing organizations (and so much in between), compassion and care for others is essential to our survival as a species. However, the notion that nurturing self and nurturing others is mutually exclusive is absurd, dangerous, and steals years of quality time from our daughters' lives—years during which they could be and *should be* thriving.

Most of us are raising pleasers without even being aware that we're doing so. We are simply raising our daughters in a way that is familiar and will allow her to "fit in" with our own (and others') socialized definition of femininity. As far as we think we've come, an acceptable woman in our patriarchal society is still quite the opposite of that fierce, confident, self-contained little girl who she came in as. Slowly, but surely, girls lose these qualities as they become shamed and ridiculed for being "bossy," "conceited," and "selfish"— and praised for being accommodating, compliant, and "nice."

As she moves through adolescence and her sense of identity is being formed, many of her "choices" will be significantly shaped by what she is told her peers want or need her to be and do (especially boys, if she is heterosexual). As Mary Pipher suggests in *Reviving Ophelia*, she may even create two versions of herself—a true and false Self that she calls upon as needed.[4] Once the powerful desire to be accepted reaches its peak in her teens, she will, in many cases, almost completely disconnect from her own wants and needs in order to please others. The desire to please leaves many girls willing to relinquish their own unique and personal desires, passions, and talents, all of which are fundamental aspects of her identity.

Nowhere have I seen this experience of giving up one's true or "authentic" Self better illustrated than in the ancient "Sealskin, Soulskin" legend, retold beautifully by Clarissa Pinkola Estés in *Women Who Run With the Wolves*. The story is about a seal woman whose sealskin is stolen by a lonely fisherman. Pleading his loneliness, he plays on her compassion and promises to return the sealskin in seven years if she will leave the sea to live with him on land. The seal woman reluctantly agrees and goes home with him. Together, the two create a child whom she loves dearly. However, over time, she becomes increasingly uncomfortable living in the outer world. Her skin becomes dry and parched, her eyelids start to peel, and her hair starts to fall out. She is essentially dying. One night she finally demands to have her sealskin back, but the husband refuses for fear that she will leave him and makes her feel guilty for being a "bad" and selfish wife and mother. Their child, initially wakened by the arguing, falls back to sleep. He awakens later to the sound of the wind calling his name, and goes out into the dark where he comes upon his mother's sealskin and returns it to her. The seal woman pulls on her sealskin, grabs her child, and heads for the ocean. She breathes into the child's mouth three times and then dives deep into the water. Together they swim deep into the sea until they arrive home with her family. In the end, however, she brings her son back to land, because it is a fundamental part of his essence, and she does not want to impose her desires or identity upon him as she had allowed her husband to do to her.[5]

The sealskin clearly symbolizes the soul, essence, identity, wisdom, courage, and self-authority with which a girl enters the world. The "outer world" of the sealskin story is the world of patriarchy that a girl begins to desire to be connected to in earnest, starting in early adolescence. Well primed by years of being taught to be a pleaser, it is as she enters and moves through adolescence that her sealskin is most likely to be taken in pieces, over time, so that she barely notices the theft. It can be and often *is* taken by parents, well-meaning friends, extended family members, and teachers who, following the patriarchal *status quo* on their own paths, take a girl's sealskin by inevitably demanding that she do the same. Of course it can also be taken by boys whom she wants to desire her, as is often the case.

Our reinforcement of "pleaser" behaviors, in concert with the various messages that communicate her lesser value as a girl, creates a debilitating combination. The typical pleaser is someone who lacks an internal compass to gauge her personal value and the value of her actions, so she is perpetually looking for validation from others. In the world of an adolescent girl, this translates as the inability to say "no" in a variety of scenarios that can have long-term consequences. She becomes so accustomed to being in tune with and accommodating the needs and desires of others that she begins to forget her own. She begins to feel lost and out of control of her life, a common precursor to stress, anxiety, cutting ("self-mutilation"), eating disorders and depression.[6] Her susceptibility to drug and alcohol use and risky sexual behavior also increases exponentially when her ability to make strong choices in the face of peer pressure feels impossible because her desire to please is so great.[7]

Perhaps most concerning is the fact that once these pleasing behaviors take hold, they are extremely difficult to change and end up being carried into adulthood. Consequently, a disproportionate number of adult people-pleasers are women.[8] In the adult world, this can mean settling for far less than they should both personally *and* professionally. The pleaser is much more likely to end up in unhealthy relationships that lack balance and equality. At work her tendency to avoid asking for a raise or promotion is much greater.[8] As mothers, if we are pleasers, we will inevitably model "pleaser" behaviors for our daughters, and the cycle continues.

The average woman usually doesn't begin to fully realize her loss of Self until she approaches her forties. There is an "awakening" that is extremely common for women at this point in our lives. It likely has something to do with slowing down for a moment after two decades of running a marathon to fulfill the patriarchal blueprint for our female lives: finish college (hopefully), maintain a romantic relationship (certainly), begin a career (probably), get married (definitely), and then have and raise babies (most definitely, or deal with being shamed and ridiculed). In the quiet stillness of this brief pause from the do-it-all chaos comes a call from deep within our being. Usually it begins as a whisper - a feeling that something important is missing and that there is a void that needs to be filled. And then, increasingly, it screams, typically in the form of rage, depression, resentment, or all of the above. It demands that she acknowledge the pit inside her where the core of her being, her truest Self, once lived and thrived when she was a little girl.

I consistently witness deeply emotional reactions when I ask a woman to recall her nine-year-old Self. My adult clients are primarily women, between the ages of thirty-five and fifty-five, and come from all walks of life. Some are stay-at-home-moms; others are artists, lawyers, managers, and business owners. Some have a high-school education and some have two or three degrees. The one thing that almost all of them have in common is the struggle to have a clear sense of their own identity and purpose. Over and over again I hear statements like "I don't feel like I know who I am" or "I know I need to create change in my life, but I'm not really sure *what* I want." These are not "heady" statements of over-privileged Western women simply facing a midlife crisis. Rather, they are statements that are symptomatic of human beings who have become so accustomed to pleasing others in order to feel acceptable, they have lost touch with their own wants, needs, and identity.

A woman's realization that she has been without her true Self for decades of her life can send her into a state of deep sadness. Ideally, she has the ability to do the work, on her own or with a therapist, to find and take back her "sealskin." This will enable her, in the second half of her life, to live not as a pleaser, but rather, as a whole individual who can live her life inspired and guided by her own needs and desires rather than someone else's. For our current generations of women (and mothers), perhaps this is the best that we can hope for.

Fortunately, we have the capacity to create a different reality for the next generation of women. Imagine a world in which our daughters won't have to wake up at forty or fifty or sixty to realize that the identity, wisdom, courage, and self-authority that they had known as little girls had been lost. Imagine what our daughters could achieve if they were encouraged to discover, know, value, and honor themselves. Imagine if they were given permission to love and nurture *themselves* first, so that they would be capable of loving and nurturing others in a healthy and balanced way, and expected nothing less in return. As parents of girls, armed with this new awareness of how and why we have been programming girls for generations, we have the ability to bring this imagined reality to fruition. If we don't, the cycle *will* continue and our girls deserve better than that. We all do.

How We Can Stop

1. **Heighten your awareness of your own journey.** If you are a woman, take some time to really process the reality of your own journey from the time when you were a girl. I always ask my adult clients to write a snapshot autobiographical timeline for themselves. Begin with your earliest memory and then record one memory for each year, until at least your twentieth year. Write down the first memory that comes to mind without questioning what comes. Once it's done, look for key transitional times in your early life. Most women will recognize shifts around the age of five, and certainly around age ten. Look for signs of moving away from your original wisdom, self-value, and identity, and toward becoming what others told you to be. Reconnecting with that little girl will not only guide you in your own deprogramming as a pleaser and start leading you back to your true Self, but it will also guide you in being that renewed person as an example for your daughter. Share your growing awareness with your partner. Ask him to do a similar exercise, and notice the differences and any similarities. This will help him to understand and work together with you to be proactive in your efforts with your daughter. Together you can explore some of the resources that I have provided below to assist you in this important work.

2. **Teach your daughter to put on her own oxygen mask first.** The thing that I love most about using this analogy with girls and women is that it helps them to see immediately how it is necessary to nurture yourself first so that you *can* nurture others. It brings into sharp focus the dangers of pleasing others first and losing yourself in the process. It allows women to be the powerful nurturers that we have the capacity and desire to be without the self-sacrificing behaviors that we are programmed to engage in as "good women." Really grasping this concept and then modeling it for your daughter will spare her the devastating price that she will pay if she becomes a pleaser. When you take "*me* time" for yourself, make sure that she knows you are doing it and why this is

important, because this will give her permission to do the same. This is no less important for your sons. Many parents are already doing it for their boys because it is an integral part of the way in which most of us teach our males to take charge of themselves so that they can, in turn, take care of others. If this sounds familiar, keep up the good work!

3. **Remember to choose wisely when it comes to bedtime stories.** Search for stories with a strong, courageous, heroic female character who lives with the balance between loving herself and loving others. This will help to give your daughter permission to do the same. I also definitely recommend learning the "Sealskin, Soulskin" story by heart and beginning to share it with her. This will enable you to have fundamentally important conversations with her about the difference between healthy and unhealthy compromise, and the importance of never sacrificing the essence of who you are for anyone.

4. **Praise your daughter's tenacity as much as you do her tenderness.** What you water will grow. Your daughter comes in with a tremendous capacity to love herself and others. She will learn to navigate both in a healthy, balanced way if she is given permission to do so and space to practice. For example, when she is really little and is determined to have a toy for herself instead of sharing, acknowledge that you understand her love for the toy and propose that she play with it first for five minutes and then share it with someone else (Notice that I did *not* say to give it to another child *first* and then take a turn.). As she gets older, when she asks challenging questions of you or her teachers, or when she expresses her dislike for something or someone who crosses her path in the world, *hear her, affirm her, and explore with her.* Dismissing or chastising her tenacious, challenging, contradictory behaviors and praising only her "pleasing" behaviors will encourage the growth of a pleaser, not a balanced human being who knows that her thoughts, feelings, desires, and passions are as valid as those of others.

5. **Compliment her intellect, creativity, leadership, and strength.** Most people instantly default to complimenting a girl's appearance. This quickly teaches her that her appearance is what is most pleasing to others. Her looks will become her primary focus, rather than the development of the qualities over which she actually has control and can assert in the world no matter what her age. Help her to refocus her attention and ask the other adults who interact with your daughter to do the same. This doesn't mean that you *don't ever* compliment her appearance. Just always make it one of many of her qualities for which you express your admiration.

6. **Get to know your daughter.** She will tell you with her questions, statements, and actions who she is and what makes her heart sing. She will even give you glimpses of the many gifts that she has brought with her to be shared with the world, if given the opportunity. As she shows you these gems, acknowledge them as important and create space for her to get really rooted in who she is, rather than asking her or telling her to be someone else. When she's young, if she expresses that she really likes a particular toy or playing a particular game, ask her what she likes about that toy or game. As she gets older, she will express her thoughts and feelings about books, movies, people in her circle, and current events. Again, talk to her about these things without judgment and without letting your own opinions dominate. This will help her to process and solidify her thoughts about what *she* likes and doesn't like, and will enable you to know her better so that you may create opportunities for her to spend more time exploring her interests (rather than the interests or expectations of others).

7. **Create opportunities for her to practice asking for what she wants.** This can be as simple as picking out what she wants to wear in the morning or ordering for herself when you go out to a restaurant. If you are always thinking, choosing, and speaking for her, she *will not* become anchored in doing so for

herself. This is a critical part of developing as an individual and believing in the value of what she thinks, desires, and vocalizes. It's equally important that she be allowed and encouraged to say "no" to whatever she doesn't want.

8. **Enroll her in a team sport.** I am a huge proponent of girls' team sports. There is room for a healthy fierceness on the field that the dance studio doesn't provide. It encourages girls to worry less about their appearance and more about the use of their mental and physical strength. As it applies to pleasing, team sports provide the ideal opportunity to practice the balance between doing well for herself *and* for others on her team. A good coach will teach her that being the best individual player that she can be will benefit her and will benefit the whole team (and, if the coach doesn't, you, as a parent, can certainly deliver this message). This is really the core message that we want our daughters to receive, so that the self-sacrificing behavior of pleasing is replaced by the self-fulfilling *and* group-fulfilling benefits of being your best Self. The icing on the cake is that she will also get the opportunity to build and experience the value of strong relationships with other girls.

9. **Become aware of your own gender-stereotype programming.** Pleasing behaviors are closely tied to many of our gender-based expectations of girls and women. Girls and boys have the capacity to be emotional *and* rational, strong *and* vulnerable, fierce *and* compassionate, self-nurturing *and* nurturing to others. Challenge every gender-based limitation you can, whether it comes from media, school, other family members, or your own programming. Think: *Girls and boys can have short hair/cook/take care of babies/fix cars/run nations.* It will make our daughters *and* our sons better, stronger, and more capable of honoring and reaching their own unique and highest potential.

Book Resources
For Women / Parents
- *I Promise Myself: Making Commitment to Yourself and Your Dreams* by Patricia Lynn Reilly
- *Imagine a Woman in Love with Herself* by Patricia Lynn Reilly
- *My Life So Far* by Jane Fonda

For Girls
- *The Paper Bag Princess* by Robert Munsch
- *Real Spirit: Fun Ideas for Refreshing, Relaxing, and Staying Strong* by Elizabeth Chobanian (American Girl)
- *Beauty: 101 Ways to Feel Great About YOU* by Therese Kauchak (American Girl)
- *Girls Rule: A Very Special Book Created Especially for Girls* by Ashley Rice

CHAPTER 9
WAY #9: FORGETTING THAT HER PATH IS HER OWN

"Your children are not your children
They are the sons and daughters of Life's longing for itself
They came through you but not from you,
And though they are with you, yet they belong not to you"
—Kahlil Gibran

What We're Doing
This final chapter won't be filled with citations of studies that support one important observation or another. It is inspired by abundant experience, razor-sharp instincts, and the wisdom of my great teachers. In many ways, it is the through line and the culmination of all the chapters that have come before it. None of the other guideposts will be fully successful if we fail at this one. Finding the courage to recognize, respect, and honor the individual paths of our girls is essential to their ability to reach their highest potential. This chapter is my deepest wish for my daughters and your daughters and, by extension, for us all.

My primary goal with my daughters and every girl I have the privilege of working with is to guide them to experience themselves as strong, confident, empowered human beings who, most importantly, believe that they are capable of creating their own paths in the world. As we've seen in the previous chapters with regard to so many other aspects of their development, most girls feel this about themselves when they are little. It is all the messages that they receive to the contrary that slowly lead them to believe that the opposite is true. At the age of seven, about the same number of boys and girls will say they want to become President. At fifteen, the number of boys remains high, but the number of girls drops dramatically.[1] Why? Because as they grow older, books, and movies don't tell them; their family traditions don't tell them; *the world around them doesn't tell them* that they are valuable and capable of creating whatever life they want *for themselves.* We certainly don't tell them they are capable of being the leader of the free world!

The socialized self-perception that they are not worthy or capable of being the captains of their own ships may be the most debilitating of all. Any human being who does not trust in her ability to create her own path will consistently wait for someone else to do it for her. She will stay stuck in difficult, damaging, and even dangerous circumstances, waiting for someone to change or "fix" them for her. She will wait for someone to rescue her, instead of rescuing herself. No wonder she doesn't think herself capable of being President; she can't even imagine herself in the leading role of her own life.

It's profoundly important to help girls develop and maintain a strong sense of personal agency, but most of us are not doing it. In large part, this is because our own deep-rooted programming tells us that the female half of our species is ill equipped. While we perceive males as being in charge of their own paths and the paths of others, we are still stuck in the flawed thinking that females are not. We don't trust women to make responsible choices for themselves *or* anyone else. If this weren't the case—if women were trusted to make thoughtful, responsible choices for themselves—the continued attempts to control women's bodies and reproductive rights would stop. If we believed that women were capable of making sound decisions for the benefit of many, the United States—allegedly one of the most progressive nations in the world—would have elected a female president by now, and women would occupy more than 18% of the seats in our government.

These realities speak volumes about our collective inability, including the inability of many women themselves, to view the female half of our species as responsible decision-makers. This is why women are hesitant to "lean in," to trust themselves, and to know that they will *be trusted* to step into leadership roles. Our centuries of programming still leads us to treat women as helpless, misguided, perpetual children. And this perspective influences our behaviors, which in turn shape the way in which our daughters see themselves. If we don't treat women as though they have this capacity, if we as women don't *embody* this capacity ourselves, how can we expect girls to know that *they have this capacity?*

Certainly, this important goal of guiding an adolescent girl to see herself as the powerful "captain of her own ship" can be complicated, challenging, and scary. Parenting effectively through adolescence must begin with a clear understanding of this important part of any human being's journey. Adolescence is the bridge between childhood and adulthood. For each and every one of us, it is a critical time of identity formation and an awakening to ourselves *as individuals*. It is a powerful call to venture out into the world and away from our parents so that we may, over time, discover and grow into autonomous beings in our own right.

Many of us have a more difficult time parenting girls through adolescence than boys. Part of this has to do with the complex and intense hormonal shifts that girls face, that we are rarely educated to understand. But I truly believe that the "white knuckling" we do with our daughters comes, more than anything, from a lack of trust in girls women to step out on their own *and* a lack of trust in the world they're stepping out into, because it so greatly undervalues them. In such a world, violence, rape, and even worse are very real concerns for women. The answer, however, must be to change our programming so that we can change the world. We must make the world's perception of girls broader, not make our girls smaller, narrower, and less than they actually are, just so that they fit into the screwed-up container *we've created*.

When parents come to me freaked out and at a loss about how to deal with their daughter's adolescent behavior, I tell them how important it is that they realize that their daughter's path is her own. She is an individual who came into this world "alone" and will leave it "alone." And, in the space between, if she is mentally and emotionally healthy, she will be naturally driven (and *should be allowed*) to discover and create a path for her own unique purpose on the planet. When you find yourself struggling, realize that she is not challenging *your* opinions when she dyes her hair pink, experiments with boys (and/or girls), or is consumed with having time with her friends. Her behavior isn't meant to hurt you—it has little or nothing to do with you. What she's doing is trying on different versions of herself and experimenting with different behaviors to figure out who she is as an individual *en route* to adulthood. Doing so is a natural and critical part of her growth into a whole human being. What makes it unhealthy (and damaging) are any overly restrictive, suffocating, or shaming reactions to her behavior.

This is something I rarely see from parents of boys. We often have one set of rules and consequences for sons and another set for daughters. Even though we have concerns about our sons being reckless, we tend to "let go" more easily and trust their journey. We allow our sons space to become individuals, because, ultimately, we believe that boys are capable of "taking care of themselves." Consequently, boys are more inclined to view themselves as capable of creating the life that they desire. Girls, on the other hand, are not socialized to believe that they have this kind of personal agency over their own happiness and success. As a result, they are more apt to dream of the man they want to marry, believing that *that's* when they'll live happily ever after. Convinced that they are incapable of steering their own ship, they end up waiting for someone else's to pick them up and sail off into the sunset.

Changing this state of learned helplessness is very much in our hands. When we show her that she is valued and we teach her how to solve problems, her self-value and confidence become firmly rooted. When we encourage her to practice making decisions, facing mistakes, and taking responsibility, she develops self-authority. When we "let go" and give her space to do all of this, with reasonable guidelines to keep her safe, we express trust in her and she thrives. And when we help her to build a filter for societal messages that threaten to compromise this foundation we have worked so diligently to create, she becomes resilient. There is no greater gift we can give our children than the ability to live healthy, joyful, independent lives in which they reach their own unique and highest potential. Why would we deny our daughters this gift?

Women are capable of creating new life in their bodies, literally allowing for the continuation of our species. How could we possibly think they aren't capable of creating their own paths? Or strong, effective governments? Or fierce yet responsible armies? Or anything that their hearts, minds, and instincts guide them to create?

How absurd it is, this patriarchal society that we have built, and how debilitating it is to us as a whole. Imagine how much greater, richer, stronger, and multifaceted it would be if we allowed our girls to become all that they have the potential to be. Imagine who they would become with the support, guidance, and space to follow the path they dreamed of when they were little. Imagine what new territory they might discover if they felt invincible long after the age of nine. Where would they take us, guided by their deep wisdom, their razor-sharp instincts, and their powerful capacity for love?

Until we peel back our own layers of programming so that we may create a world in which girls and women can truly thrive along side our male counterparts, we'll never know....

How We Can Stop

1. **Peel back your own layers.** You know the drill by now. You can't teach to your children that which you don't know well enough to embody yourself. Think about the obstacles that sat (and perhaps still sit) in the way of creating the life you desired. Identify them and then create a plan for removing them one by one. The opportunity for your daughter to see you doing so, especially if you share with her what you are doing and why, will be a great source of inspiration to her. Be highly conscious of not allowing these same boulders to be placed on your daughter's path.

2. **Always remember the ultimate goal of parenting.** Remind yourself that, while you will always be there for her, your goal is for her to one day not *need* you. Her path is her own. Provide her with abundant information and tools, and provide space for her to practice with both. Both of my daughters became responsible for making their own beds at the age of five. I taught my older daughter how to do her own laundry when she was nine (the same age at which my mother taught my brother and me), and she has been making her own lunch for school since she was ten (with certain guidelines based on the lunch ingredients I keep in the house). It would have been easier for her (and sometimes for me, too) if I had continued to do these things for her. However, there is absolutely no question that being in charge of these things for herself,

knowing that I believed that she was capable of handling them, has inspired the sense of confidence and independence that she has today. These fundamental gifts to your daughter will enable her to provide for herself, in a variety of ways. This is one of the greatest sources of empowerment that you could ever give her.

3. **Provide opportunities to see herself as the captain of her own ship.** It begins with allowing her to choose what she wants to wear to school and the book she wants you to read to her at bedtime. These simple choices will translate into much bigger decision-making abilities as she gets older because she will have developed these "internal muscles" and become familiar with what it feels like to steer her ship. You will have to remind her that, for her own wellbeing, her parents will have the final say on many issues. However, if, you think of yourself as a guide and give her many opportunities to make her own choices, by the time she leaves the nest, you will all feel more confident that she is able to handle important decision-making on her own. Just keep reminding yourself that if she only knows how to move through the world with someone else at the helm, she will always just replace one "captain" (such as her parents) with another (domineering friends, boyfriends, girlfriends, a husband, etc.).

4. **Help her to become a problem-solver.** As individuals, we become capable of handling life's challenges by practicing doing so. We do our children a great disservice when we either shelter them or fix everything for them. When your daughter faces a challenge, take the opportunity to *guide* her through identifying the problem, creating a solution, and implementing it. When she's young, this may apply to cleaning up a mess that she's made, or putting together a puzzle. As she gets a little older, it will more likely apply to dealing with a teacher whom she doesn't like, or navigating relationship conflicts. In any case, consistently reminding her to apply these three problem-solving steps will be fundamentally

empowering for her, because the likelihood of her giving up when she faces adversity or getting stuck in situations that are unhealthy for her is significantly diminished.

5. **Provide her with take-charge role models.** Because there are so many messages that she gets about women *not being in charge of themselves,* whenever possible, she needs to see clear examples in her life that demonstrate the opposite. It is especially critical that your daughter see her mom as someone who takes charge of her own life, her own decision-making, and her own problem-solving. These role models can also be introduced through carefully chosen books and movies, some of which I have listed below. Whatever the source, it's essential to give her an example that she can follow. Remember that she can't be what she can't see.

6. **Make family dinners a priority.** Set a precedent when she is young that will carry on throughout her adolescence. Family dinner-table conversations can be some of the least threatening and, therefore, most fruitful ways to have regular dialogue about what is going on in her day. Get her comfortable telling you about her struggles by listening intently and without judgment, and then provide gentle guidance regarding how *she* can find solutions to problems. When she shares her triumphs, celebrate her accomplishments. If she's used to talking openly with you at seven, there will be a stronger foundation for talking about bigger issues when she's fourteen.

7. **Let your son be your guide.** If you would do it for him, do it for her. This is a great rule of thumb for parents who have both boys and girls. Make an important shift in how you raise your daughter by extending the same perceptions of strength, courage, strong decision-making, and leadership to her as you would to your son. It will provide the space she needs, demonstrate your confidence in her, and make strong statements about gender equality in your household.

Book Resources
For Young Girls

- *The Paper Bag Princess* by Robert Munsch
- *Girls Rule...A Very Special Book Created Especially for Girls* by Ashley Rice
- *You Can Be a Woman Engineer* by Judith Love Cohen
- *You Can Be a Woman Zoologist* by Valerie Thompson and Judith Love Cohen
- *You Can Be a Woman Video Game Producer* by Judith Love Cohen
- *You Can Be a Woman Paleontologist* by Diane L. Gabriel and Judith Love Cohen
- *You Can Be a Woman Egyptologist* by Betsy M. Bryan and Judith Love Cohen

These books are part of a brilliant and groundbreaking series that emphasizes the value and ability of women who created their own paths by working in various fields not traditionally filled by women. The books depict the lives of real women whose careers provide inspirational role models. Others include *You Can Be a Woman Architect, Marine Biologist, Astronomer, Cardiologist, Oceanographer, and Botanist.*

For Adolescent Girls

- *I Am An Emotional Creature* by Eve Ensler
- *The Thundering Years: Rituals and Sacred Wisdom for Teens* by Julie Tallard Johnson
- *The Goddess in Every Girl: Develop Your Teen Feminine Power* by M.J. Abadie

Online

- *A Mighty Girl* - The world's largest collection of books, toys and movies for smart, confident, and courageous girls (*www.amightygirl.com*).
- *New Moon Girls* is an inspirational magazine and online site for girls ages eight and up to engage in self-discovery, creativity, and community (http://www.newmoon.com/)

Workshops and Camps

- REALgirl Empowerment Programs: Unique and innovative programs dedicated to inspiring and guiding girls to discover their "real" (authentic) selves. It is our goal to provide essential life skills that every girl/young woman needs for healthy maturation, development, formation of healthy relationships, and the opportunity to reach her own unique and highest potential. Through art, movement (yoga and dance), discussion, writing, theatre games, guest speakers, and a variety of other dynamic activities, participants will be guided to develop tools to successfully navigate issues that every girl faces today. To find a camp near you, visit: www.realgirlprograms.com

SOURCES

Introduction

1. Gurian, Anita. "How to Raise Girls with Healthy Self-esteem." *NYU Child Study Center.* 2009. http://www.aboutourkids.org/articles/how_raise_girls_healthy_selfesteem

2. *Ibid.*

3. Smith, Gabie E., Meg Gerrard and Frederick X. Gibbons. "Self-Esteem and the Relation Between Risk Behavior and Perceptions of Vulnerability to Unplanned Pregnancy in College Women," *Health Psychology,* 16, no. 2,(1997), 137-146.

Chapter 1

1. Hesse-Biber, Sharlene Nagy, ed., *Feminist Research Practice: A Primer.* Thousand Oaks, California: Sage Publications, 2007.

2. Scherman, Nosson. *The Complete ArtScroll Siddur.* Morning Blessings. Page 12.

3. Hyman, Paula E. "The Introduction of Bat Mitzvah in Conservative Judaism in Postwar America." *YIVO Annual* 19 (1990), 133-146.

4. Fiona Govan, "Ordaining women is 'crime,' says Vatican," *The Gazette,* July 15, 2010, http://www.montrealgazette.com/news/Ordaining+women+crime+says+Vatican/3281506/story.html

5. Cindy Wooden, "Evangelii Gaudium: Pope says only men can be priests, but women must have voice in Church," *Catholic Herald,* November 26, 2013, http://www.catholicherald.co.uk/news/2013/11/26/evangelii-gaudium-pope-says-only-men-can-be-priests-but-women-must-have-voice-in-church/

6. Offen, Karen. "A Brief History of Marriage," International Museum of Women, http://imow.org/economica/stories/viewStory?storyId=3650

7. U.S. Const., amend. XIX.

8. "The Equal Rights Amendment," http://www.equalrightsamendment.org/ January 15, 2014.

9. Criminal Law – The Husband's Rape Exemption: An Equal Protection Alternative. (1977). Available at http://assets.wne.edu/159/28_note_Criminal.pdf **This is a criminal law paper written about the case *State v. Smith* that overturned the law that allows husbands to rape their wives.

10. "Women in Congress," Center for American Women and Politics, http://www.cawp.rutgers.edu/fast_facts/levels_of_office/documents/cong.pdf

11. Karen Tumulty. "Nancy Pelosi and the newsmags: What about all the cover stories? Wait, there aren't any," *Washington Post*, April 5, 2012, http://www.washingtonpost.com/blogs/she-the-people/post/re-isnt-it-time-what-about-all-those-speaker-pelosi-cover-stories-wait--there-werent-any/2012/04/05/gIQAtKunxS_blog.html

12. Smith, Stacy L. and Mark Choueiti. "Gender Disparity on Screen and Behind the Camera in Family Films; The Executive Report." USC Annenberg School for Communication and Journalism, http://annenberg.usc.edu/Faculty/Communication%20and%20Journalism/~/media/3555BE381A4541949D0AB8C234A1B7DB.ashx January 15th, 2014

13. "The Representation Project," http://www.missrepresentation.org/about-us/resources/gender-resources/ January 15th, 2014

14. Geena Davis Institute on Gender in Media, http://www.seejane.org/research/ January 15th, 2014

15. Jo Rowling, interview by Oprah Winfrey, *The Oprah Winfrey Show*, October 1, 2010.

16. Clark, Roger, Kieran Ayton, Nicole Frechette, and Pamela J. Keller, "Women of the World Re-Write! Women in American World History High School Textbooks from the 1960s, 1980s, and 1990s." *Social Education* Vol 69 (2005).

17. Applebee, Arthur N. (1989). A Study of Book-Length Works Taught

in High School English Programs. Albany, NY: Center for Learning and Teaching of Literature. http://www.csun.edu/~krowlands/Content/Academic_Resources/Literature/Canon/Applebee-Book%20length%20works.pdf

18. Powell, R. R., & J. Garcia, "The Portrayal of Minorities and Women in Selected Elementary Science Series." *Journal of Research in Science Teaching*, Vol 22, 519–533.

Chapter 2

1. "Profile America Facts for Features: How Many Fathers?" US Census Bureau, 2013, http://www.census.gov/newsroom/releases/archives/facts_for_features_special_editions/cb13-ff13.html

2. Hesse-Biber, Sharlene Nagy, ed., *Feminist Research Practice: A Primer*. Thousand Oaks, California: Sage Publications, 2007.

3. Mary Zeiss Stange, "A Dance for Chastity," *USA Today*, March 18, 2007, http://usatoday30.usatoday.com/news/opinion/2007-03-18-purity-revolution_N.htm

4. Sharpe, S. *Fathers and Daughters*. New Fetterlane, London: Routledge, 1994.

5. Orava, Tammy A., Peter J. McLeod, & Donald Sharpe. "Perceptions of Control, Depressive Symptomatology, and Self-Esteem of Women in Transition from Abusive Relationships," *Journal of Family Violence* Volume 11, Issue 2 (1996), 167-186. http://link.springer.com/article/10.1007/BF02336668.

6. Porter, Anthony. "A Call to Men." TedTalk. Washington, D.C. December 2010. Conference presentation.

7. Steele, Claude. "A Threat in the Air: How Stereotypes Shape Intellectual Identity and Performance," *American Psychologist*. Vol 52(6) (1997), 613-629. http://psycnet.apa.org/journals/amp/52/6/613/

8. Scheffler, Tanya and Peter J. Naus. "The Relationship Between Fatherly Affirmation and a Woman's Self-Esteem, Fear of Intimacy, Comfort with Womanhood, and Comfort with Sexuality," *The Canadian Journal of Human Sexuality*, 8, no. 1 (1999). 39-45, http://www.canadiancrc.com/Fatherlessness/Relationship_Between_Fatherly_Affirmation_and_

Woman_Self-Esteem_Fear_Intimacy_Womanhood_Sexuality-Scheffer_
Naus_1999.aspx#Sharpe

Chapter 3

1. England, Paula. "The Gender Revolution: Uneven and Stalled." *Gender & Society* 24, no.2 (2010), 149-166.

2. Gurian, Anita. "Gifted Girls – Many Gifted Girls, Few Eminent Women: Why?" NYU Child Study Center, http://www.aboutourkids.org/articles/gifted_girls_many_gifted_girls_few_eminent_women_why

3. Davis, Antoinette, MPH, "Interpersonal and Physical Dating Violence among Teens," The National Council on Crime and Delinquency, January 15th, 2014. http://www.nccdglobal.org/sites/default/files/publication_pdf/focus-dating-violence.pdf

4. "Intimate Partner Violence in the United States, 1993-2004," Department of Justice, Bureau of Justice Statistics, December 2006 http://www.bjs.gov/content/pub/pdf/ipvus.pdf

5. Foshee, V.A, G.F. Linder, K.E. Bauman, *et al.* "The Safe Dates Project: Theoretical Basis, Evaluation Design, and Selected Baseline Findings." *American Journal of Preventative Medicine* 12, no. 2 (1996), 39-47.

6. Silverman, J., A. Raj, *et al.* "Dating Violence Against Adolescent Girls and Associated Substance Use, Unhealthy Weight Control, Sexual Risk Behavior, Pregnancy, and Suicidality." *JAMA* Vol 286 (2001), 572-579, http://jama.amaassn.org/cgi/reprint/286/5/572

7. Decker, M., J, Silverman, A. Raj. "Dating Violence and Sexually Transmitted Disease/HIV Testing and Diagnosis Among Adolescent Females." *Pediatrics* Vol 116 (2005), 272-276.

8. Liz Claiborne, Inc., Conducted by Teen Research Unlimited. (February 2005). http://www.clotheslineproject.org/teendatingviolencefacts.pdf

Chapter 4

1. "Containment." Def. 1. *Oxford Dictionary Online*. Oxford Dictionary. Web. 24 March 2014.

2. Patel, A.N., E. Park, M. Kuzman, F.J Silva, and JG Allickson. "Multipotent Menstrual Blood Stromal Stem Cells: Isolation, Characterization, and Differentiation." *Cell Transplantation*. Vol 17 (2008) 313-311. Also Rahimi, M., H. Mohseni-Kouchesfahani, S. Mobini, S. Nikoo, A.H. Zarnani, S. Kazemnejad (2014). "Evaluation of Menstrual Blood Stem Cells Seeded in Biocompatible *Bombyx Mori* Silk Fibroin Scaffold for Cardiac Tissue Engineering." J Biomater Appl. [Epub ahead of print].

3. Shaun Dreisbach, "Shocking Body-Image News: 97% of Women Will Be Cruel to Their Bodies Today," *Glamour*, February 2011, http://www.glamour.com/health-fitness/2011/02/shocking-body-image-news-97-percent-of-women-will-be-cruel-to-their-bodies-today.

4. Rembeck, Gun. *The Winding Road to Womanhood*. University of Gothenburg, 2008, 9.

5. Costos, Daryl, Ruthie Ackerman, and Lisa Paradis. "Recollections of Menarche: Communication Between Mothers and Daughters Regarding Menstruation." *Sex Roles* Vol 46 Issue 1-2 (2002) 49-59

6. Rembeck, Gun. *The Winding Road to Womanhood*. University of Gothenburg, 2008, 9.

7. Scheffler, Tanya & Peter J. Naus. "The Relationship Between Fatherly Affirmation and a Woman's Self-Esteem, Fear of Intimacy, Comfort with Womanhood, and Comfort with Sexuality." *The Canadian Journal of Human Sexuality*, 8, no.1 (1999):39-45. http://www.canadiancrc.com/Fatherlessness/Relationship_Between_Fatherly_Affirmation_and_Woman_Self-Esteem_Fear_Intimacy_Womanhood_Sexuality-Scheffer_Naus_1999.aspx#Sharpe

8. Press, Zoë. "Menstruation, Emissions, and Holy Communion." *Orthodox Christian Information Center*. Web. 24 March 2014.

9. Moore, John. *Lovebite: Mythology and the Semiotics of Culture*. London: Apporia Press. (1990) Web. January 15, 2014.

10. "State Policies on Sex Education in Schools," National Conference of

State Legislatures, 2014, http://www.ncsl.org/research/health/state-policies-on-sex-education-in-schools.aspx

11. "Legacy." *Southland*. TNT. Los Angeles. 14 February 2012. Television.

12. Roberts, Tomi-Ann, Jaime L. Goldenberg, Cathleen Power, and Dr. Tom Pyszczynski "Feminine Protection": The Effects of Menstruation on Attitudes of Women." *Psychology of Women Quarterly*, 26. (2002), 131-139. http://www.academia.edu/2096344/_Feminine_Protection_The_Effects_of_Menstruation_on_Attitudes_Toward_Women

13. Forbes, Gordon, Leah Adams-Curtis, Kay White, and Katie Holmgren "The Role of Hostile and Benevolent Sexism in Women's and Men's Perceptions of the Menstruating Woman" *Psychology of Women Quarterly*. Vol 27 Issue 1 (2003), 58-63. http://pwq.sagepub.com/content/27/1/58.abstract

14. Kessler, Kelly L. *Self-Objectification, Body Image, Eating Behaviors, and Exercise Dependence among College Females* Denton, Texas. UNT Digital Library. (2010),http://digital.library.unt.edu/ark:/67531/metadc30477/m2/1/high_res_d/thesis.pdf. Accessed January 15, 2014.; Also Muehlenkamp, Jennifer J. & Amy M. Brausch "Body Image as a Mediator of Non-Suicidal Self-Injury" (2012), *Journal of Adolescence*. Vol. 35 pp. 1-9. http://www.selfinjury.bctr.cornell.edu/perch/resources/body-image.pdf.

15. Denmark, Florence & Michele Antoinette Paludi *Psychology of Women: A Handbook of Issues and Theories*. Westport, Connecticut: Praeger, 2008, 415

16. Rembeck, Gun. *The Winding Road to Womanhood*. University of Gothenburg, 2008, 9.

17. "Yoni." *AskDefine: The Collaborative Dictionary*. Web. 24 March 2014.

18. Witherspoon, Gary. Language and Art in the Navajo Universe. University of Michigan Press. (1977). Cited in online article http://xroads.virginia.edu/~ma97/dinetah/change2.html

19. Grahn, Judy. *Blood, Bread, and Roses: How Menstruation Created the World*. Boston: Beacon Press, 1994.

20. Hussain, A and F. Ahsan "The Vagina as a Route for Systemic Drug

Delivery." *Journal of Controlled Release*. Vol 103 (2005), 301-313.

Chapter 5

1. Alford, S. *et al.* "Science and Success: Sex Education and Other Programs that Work to Prevent Teen Pregnancy, HIV & Sexually Transmitted Infections. Washington, DC." Advocates for Youth, 2008, http://www.advocatesforyouth.org/publications/367?task=view

2. Tolman, Deborah L. *Dilemmas of Desire: Teenage Girls Talk about Sexuality.* Cambridge, Massachusetts: Harvard University Press, 2002, 3.

3. Decker, M., J. Silverman, A Raj. "Dating Violence and Sexually Transmitted Disease/HIV Testing and Diagnosis among Adolescent Females." *Pediatrics*, Vol 116 (2005): 272-276.

4. Jackson, Sandy & Goossens, Luc, eds. *The Handbook of Adolescent Development.* Hove, United Kingdom: Psychology Press. 2006.

5. Office of the Surgeon General (US). "The Surgeon General's Call to Action to Promote Sexual Health and Responsible Sexual Behavior," Rockville (MD): The Office of the Surgeon General (US) 2001, http://www.ncbi.nlm.nih.gov/books/NBK44223/

6. Wolf, Naomi. *Promiscuities: The Secret Struggle for Womanhood.* New York: Ballantine Books, 1998.

7. Rembeck, Gun. *The Winding Road to Womanhood.* University of Gothenburg, 2008, 7.

8. Hibbard, Laura. "Ashlynn Conner, 10-years-old, Hanged Herself After Bullying, Parents Say." *Huffington Post Online.* 14 November 2011. Web. 24 March 2014.

9. Salazar, L.F., R.A Crosby, R.J. DiClemente, G.M. Wingood, C.M. Lescano, L.K. Brown, K. Harrington, S. Davies "Self-Esteem and Theoretical Mediators of Safer Sex among African American Female Adolescents: Implications for Sexual Risk Reduction Interventions," *Health, Education and* Behavior. Vol 32 Issue 3. 2005, 413-427. http://www.ncbi.nlm.nih.gov/pubmed/15851547

Chapter 6

1. Smith, Stacy. Gender Inequality in 500 Popular Films: Examining On-Screen Portrayals and Behind-the-Scenes Employment Patterns in Motion Pictures Released between 2007-2012.", 2013, USC Annenberg School for Communication and Journalism,http://annenberg.usc.edu/Faculty/Communication%20and%20Journalism/~/media/5D B47326757B416FBE2CB5E6F1B5CBE4.ashx

2. *Ibid.*

3. *Ibid.*

4. Hawkins, Nicole. "The Media Myths: Understanding the Pressure Placed on Women to be Perfect," 2011, https://socialwork.byu.edu/SiteAssets/News%20and%20Events/PowerPoint%20Dr.%20Nicole%20Hawkins%20Lecture.pdf

5. Corydon Ireland. "Fijian girls succumb to Western Dysmorphia," *The Harvard Gazette.* March 2009, http://news.harvard.edu/gazette/story/2009/03/fijian-girls-succumb-to-western-dysmorphia/

6. Goode, Erica. "Study Finds TV Alters Fiji Girls' View of Body." *The New York Times,* May 20, 1999, http://www.nytimes.com/1999/05/20/world/study-finds-tv-alters-fiji-girls-view-of-body.html

7. "Women in Peril: A Look at TV's Disturbing New Storyline Trend" Parents Television Council, 2009, https://www.parentstv.org/PTC/publications/reports/womeninperil/study.pdf

8. Thompson, J. Kevin and Leslie Heinberg. "The Media's Influence on Body Image Disturbance and Eating Disorders: We've Reviled Them, Now Can We Rehabilitate Them?" 1999, http://198.199.127.24/thumbs/7e9b6938fe6ead79c76db02ab70be0b1.pdf

9. *Taylor Kids Pulse: Where the Wired Things Are,* The Taylor Research & Consulting Group (2003)as cited in *Teen Media Monitor: Teen Girls,* The Kaiser Family Foundation 2, no. 1

10. Duke, Lisa and Peggy Kreshel. (1998). "Negotiating Femininity: Girls in Early Adolescence Read Teen Magazines." *Journal of Communication Inquiry* 22, no. 1 (1998): 48-72. Study quoted in web article, available at http://kaiserfamilyfoundation.files.wordpress.

com/2013/01/tweens-teens-and-magazines-fact-sheet.pdf

11. *Seventeen Magazine.* (July 2009). 26-28.

12. *Seventeen Magazine.* (July 2009). 112-115.

13. Tiggemann, Marika. "Media Exposure, Body Dissatisfaction and Disordered Eating: Television and Magazines are Not the same!" *European Eating Disorders Review.* Vol 11, Issue 5 (2003), 418-430. http://onlinelibrary.wiley.com/doi/10.1002/erv.502/abstract

14. Stice, Eric Erika Schupak-Neuberg, Heather Shaw, Richard. "Relation of Media Exposure to Eating Disorder Symptomatology: An Examination of Mediating Mechanisms" *Journal of Abnormal Psychology.* Vol 103 Issue 4 (1994), 836-840. http://psycnet.apa.org/index.cfm?fa=search.displayRecord&uid=1995-10029-001

15. *Ibid.*

16. Tiggemann, M., & B McGill: "The Role of Social Comparison in the Effect of Magazine Advertisements on Women's Mood and Body Dissatisfaction." *Journal of Social & Clinical Psychology* (2004), http://jkthompson.myweb.usf.edu/articles/Media%20exposure%20mood%20and%20body%20image%20dissatisfaction.pdf

17. Tiggemann, Marika. "Media Exposure, Body Dissatisfaction and Disordered Eating: Television and Magazines are Not the same!" (2003), http://onlinelibrary.wiley.com/doi/10.1002/erv.502/abstract

18. Schooler, Deborah, L. Monique Ward, Ann Merriweather and Allison Caruthers: "Who's That Girl: Television's Role in the Body Image Development of Young White and Black Women." *Psychology of WomenQuarterly* (2003),http://pwq.sagepub.com/content/28/1/38. abstract

19. The Mayo Clinic. "Children and TV: Limiting your Child's Screen Time,"http://www.mayoclinic.org/children-and-tv/art-20047952?pg=1 January 15, 2014

20. *Ibid.*

Chapter 7

1. Sadker, Myra, David Sadker, and Karen Zittleman *Still Failing at Fairness: How Gender Bias Cheats Girls and Boys in School and What We Can Do About It.* New York: Simon & Schuster, 2009. 125.

2. Orenstein, Peggy. *SchoolGirls: Young Women, Self-esteem, and the Confidence Gap.* New York: Anchor Books, 1994.

3. *Ibid.*

4. Sadker, Myra, David Sadker, and Karen Zittleman *Still Failing at Fairness: How Gender Bias Cheats Girls and Boys in School and What We Can Do About It.* New York: Simon & Schuster, 2009. 125.

5. Bogue, Anea, Karen Fox and Lauren Stower, "Gender Parity in the Middle School Classroom" (2014).

6. Dweck, C. S., Goetz, T. E., & Strauss, N. L. (1980). Sex differences in learned helplessness: An experimental and naturalistic study of failure generalization and its mediators. Journal of Personality and Social Psychology, 38(3), 441-452.

7. *Ibid.*

8. *Ibid.*

9. Orenstein, Peggy. *SchoolGirls: Young Women, Self-esteem, and the Confidence Gap.* New York: Anchor Books, 1994.

10. *Ibid.*

11. Bogue, Anea, Karen Fox and Lauren Stower, "Gender Parity in the Middle School Classroom" (2014).

12. Black, Linda Jones. "Textbooks, Gender, and World History," 2012, http://www.historycooperative.org/journals/whc/3.2/black.html.

13. *Ibid.*

14. Bogue, Anea, Karen Fox and Lauren Stower, "Gender Parity in the Middle School Classroom" (2014).

15. Good, Jessica J., Julie A. Woodzicka, and Lylan C. Wingfield "The Effects of Gender Stereotypic and Counter-Stereotypic Textbook Images on Science Performance, 2010, http://legacy.earlham.

edu/~pardhan/research/refs/effect_of_stereotypes.pdf

16. Bazler, Judith A. & Doris A. Simonis: "Are High School Chemistry Textbooks Gender Fair?" 2006, http://onlinelibrary.wiley.com/doi/10.1002/tea.3660280408/abstract

17. Good, Jessica J., Julie A. Woodzicka, and Lylan C. Wingfield "The Effects of Gender Stereotypic and Counter-Stereotypic Textbook Images on Science Performance, 2010, http://legacy.earlham.edu/~pardhan/research/refs/effect_of_stereotypes.pdf

18. *Ibid.*

19. *Ibid.*

20. Powell, R. R., and J. Garcia: "The Portrayal of Minorities and Women in Selected Elementary science Series." *Journal of Research in Science Teaching*, Vol 22 (1985), 519–533.

21. Elena Novak. "Top 7 Master's Degrees for Making the Most Money." *The Huffington Post,* , October 3, 2013,"http://www.huffingtonpost.com/uloop/top-7-masters-degrees-for-making-money_b_4036525.html.

22. "STEM Learning in Afterschool: An Analysis of Impact and Outcomes," Afterschool Alliance, 2011,http://www.afterschoolalliance.org/STEM-Afterschool-Outcomes.pdf.

23. "Women's Educational Equity Act" National Alliance for Partnerships in Equity, 2013 http://www.napequity.org/public-

Chapter 8

1. Reilly, Patricia Lynn. *Imagine a Woman in Love with Herself.* York Beach (ME): Conari Press, 1998.

2. "The Supergirl Dilemma: Girls Grapple with the Mounting Pressure of Expectations," Girls Inc., 2006, http://www.thefreelibrary.com/The+Supergirl+Dilemma%3A+Girls+Feel+the+Pressure+to+Be+Perfect,...-a0152752222

3. "Oprah's Master Class with Jane Fonda" OWN Network, 2012, http://www.oprah.com/own-master-class/Oprahs-Master-Class-

Jane-Fonda.

4. Pipher, Mary. *Reviving Ophelia*. New York (NY): Penguin Group, Inc., 1994.

5. Estés, Clarissa Pinkola. *Women Who Run with the Wolves*. New York: The Random House Publishing Group, 1996.

6. Curtis, Carolyn A. "Self-Destructive Behaviors of Adolescent Girls and Boys." Honors Thesis, 2008. Colby College. Paper 295. http://digitalcommons.colby.edu/honorstheses/295

7. *Ibid.*

8. Svoboda, Elizabeth. "Field Guide to the People-Pleaser: May I Serve As Your Doormat?" *Psychology Today*, 2008, http://www.psychology-today.com/articles/200805/field-guide-the-people-pleaser-may-i-serve-your-doormat

Chapter 9

1. *Miss Representation*, Jennifer Siebel Newsom (Film Director), and Founder & CEO of Girls Club Entertainment

ABOUT THE AUTHOR

Anea Bogue, B.Ed., M.A. is an acclaimed self-esteem expert and researcher specializing in the empowerment of girls and women. The mother of 17-year-old and 5-year-old daughters, Anea is absolutely passionate about her work and has dedicated more than half her life to this cause.

Her more than 20 years of experience include her work as an educator, counselor, consultant, author, speaker and creator of REALgirl®, a revolutionary empowerment program for girls. Anea also recently co-founded TrueMoon®, a feminine care company dedicated to providing safe, healthy products, and positive, informative messaging for girls and women about their bodies. Anea is committed to helping each girl and woman discover her authentic self and reach her highest potential. She currently lives in Los Angeles with her family. To learn more about Anea please visit www.AneaBogue.com.